PSYCHOLOGICAL DISORDER SIMPLY EXPLAINED:

A Guide for Everyone

Ted Brooke

TABLE OF CONTENTS

INTRODUCTION

Before we start, we should do a misrepresented relationship with our reality. In a warrior society, a caring individual who is a Buddhist (with great serotonin/dopamine creation in his mind) would be analyzed by warrior clinicians to experience the ill effects of "weakness disorder" and may be treated with alcohol. So also in a benevolently amicable Buddhist society, a forceful warrior would be analyzed as having a type of hostile to a social issue and treated with whatever the priest therapists esteem legitimate.

In Myers Briggs character typology depictions, one can channel the most versatile and maladaptive qualities of each kind. Accepting the sort we're taking a gander at is an intense one (state an ESTP with each letter being 60 or over), the supposed "positives" and "negatives" can be separated rapidly. It, at that point, turns out to be naturally intelligent to believe that some MBTI types are bound to have some mental "issue" than others depending on their default methods of being. Each of the ones needs to do is coordinate the portrayals of psych issue with depictions of MBTI types when they are not at their best and can't bargain (say a worrying low salary and low instruction INFP in a nation where ESTJs overwhelm socially and anticipate that everyone should resemble them). The motivation behind why I put psych "scatters" into quote marks is that as indicated over, these maladaptive "conditions" have all the earmarks of being (generally) physiological attributes of various types of homo sapien when they are headed to the psychotic limit by social conditions. Negative brain research still overwhelms and possibly orders conditions when they become the most evident and serious. Generally, that includes a specific type of individual on a lower end of the financial scale, which is constrained to look for help to keep working. The counterproductive idea of negative brain research (versus the developing field of positive brain research) has been doing hurt for over a century now.

At the end of the day,

1) The prevailing society/financial arrangement of a nation is frequently firmly corresponded to a couple of predominant Myers Briggs types (outgoing Ts for the most part) [0]

2) Breeds that physiologically contrast from the group's decision breeds are constrained to take an interest in a financial framework (run by the rulers) that is contrary to them

3) If individuals who are incongruent with their framework are well off and associated, they have additional methods for dealing with stress to manage stressors and maintain a strategic distance from/diminish actuation of their MBTI type's "negative" psychotic characteristics

4) Those breeds liable to look for help (and have their condition characterized and classified as science) have had the positive characteristics of their MBTI type smothered and negative ones overstated by the despondency causing social stressors. They are

probably going to be from the less fortunate less taught finish of the low class and in this way to have more on their plates every day while not having the option to verbalize whats sickly them too. Regardless of whether they are from the self-important working-class group that likes itself as a "white-collar class," they are still prone to be misled about the key auxiliary nature of their mental issues and concede to the supposed specialists inside the enterprise commanded field of negative brain research.

5) All of this is exacerbated when the monetary pie is contracting as opposed to extending (this implies an inversion of industrialization instead of the consistent material reestablishment of an industrialized nation).We should begin the adventure towards coordinating what Myers-Briggs breeds are bound to get a specific "issue" characterization for one of their progressively outrageous individuals. As a benchmark, the MBTI types to be coordinated are intense ones (60 or more on each letter). A few issues may require just one capacity to be anomalous (measurably) high, for

example, 100 F. In this manner, not all intense MBTI types would fundamental match issue depictions, yet those intense MBTI types inside the effectively intense pool of their brethren. This is an inadequate and flawed rundown that will be updated as time goes on. It is to fill in as a beginning stage for exchange.

Mental imbalance Spectrum

Almost certain among ISTPs - The high Sensing capacity of near 100 appears to be key as the nerves prompting the eyeballs are thicker than in a great many people. Sanctuary Grandin, a mentally unbalanced lady, clarified superbly in her TED discourse that she "thinks" in pictures as opposed to emblematically. She entertainingly makes reference to that the contemplative researchers/creators/specialists in the group of spectators are most likely contacting the limit of chemical imbalance at times, and that encourages them in their detail explicit work. The high Introversion clarifies the very low relational abilities and shirking of social circumstances that are vitality depleting for the medically introverted. The high T and coldness clarify the absence of close connection to objects inside the world during those uncommon occasions when the mentally unbalanced individual decides to draw in with the world (a blip of extroversion). The high P adds to the loss of motion of activity and too tangible over-burden. The mind is most likely overclocked with video/sound contributions without an organic method to pleasingly use the information. The general outcome is an individual acting particularly like someone on dissociative medications (fit for being nearest to consummate automated target impression of the world without feeling obfuscating it). Temperament Disorders - Depressive and Bipolar (For enthusiastic crazy rides to occur in any case, one needs a too solid F work (again 90-100 territory) to feel the outrageous highs just as the extraordinary lows. Different capacities decide the particular mindset issue at work.)

Gloom

Almost certain among ISFJs and ESFJs - Our current ENTJ/ENTP ruled society is antagonistic to the generous SFJs. Quick, innovative and social change, atomization of society and family by a free market, and the no-nonsense relational collaborations are the well on the way to have the most noteworthy negative effect on SFJs. Their supportiveness isn't remunerated yet disparaged and compelled by a sense of honor SFJs are more averse to unwind and party like their FP partners. Solid S makes them center around their consistent absence of certification by others in the present time and place while the J adds to a rigid and genuinely charged moralistic framework that is always observed by the S as being damaged. Solid J additionally grapples the individual in a discouraged agonizing state of mind with fewer interferences into a more joyful, increasingly raised mode (see underneath).

Bipolar

More probable among the ENFPs and ESFPs - Considering the hyper outgoing period of a bipolar individual, the high E seems a key contributor alongside the exceptionally high F. The high P adds to the quick exchanging of states of mind and their wildness (differentiated to long constant agonizing on a specific passionate plane by a solid J). The outgoing FP goes towards the world brimming with vitality and motivation; however, it gets shot somewhere around the negative social condition. Intense affectability to analysis and a solid P to see how such analysis is justified from numerous points makes a serious enthusiastic breakdown and withdrawal into a burdensome stage. The steady, enthusiastic changing adds to mental perplexity and feeling of absence of control. These are the individuals who love to party and are everywhere except face serious accidents while experiencing a natural snag. Extroversion must be kept up and not restrained horribly.

ADHD

Almost certain among ENFPs, ESFPs, ENTPs, and ESTPs - Key has all the earmarks of being consistent exchanging of keen points by a P more than 60 and solid extroversion that causes the individual to go towards the world and feel dulled when that longing is baffled. Likewise has all the earmarks of being only a typical youth investigation period of babies and offspring of most MBTI types.

Schizoid Personality

More probable among ISTJs, INTJs, and potentially INTPs - Schizoids are set apart by social segregation, enthusiastic frigidity, and lack of concern to other people. Impaired social working, extraordinary dejection, and bombastic dreams of extroversion. The above qualities are clearly brought about by the same solid I and T as in the medically introverted, yet the schizoids are not completely overburdened with a tactile over-burden. This enables them to be inventive on occasion. Political Ponerology puts forth an intriguing defense that Schizoids (because of them investing loads of energy alone taking a gander at the quick-moving world with frequently vindictive dreams) compose the writing and builds that motivates subclinical and clinical insane people.

Psychopathy

Almost certain among ENTJs, ENTPs - These are human group's normal predators and devour it in the event that they get into control as opposed to improving it. The fundamental components are the greatest high T of 100 for clinical mental cases and a T more than 60 for subclinical ones (the milder ones who have a foot in both the human world and the savage world and who make common legislators). This ensures there is no passionate compassion for individual homo sapien. They actually can't feel the manner in which others feel, and this makes a great many people appear to be unreasonable and powerless to them. The nearest they need to feel (that they mistake the idea for) is sexual excitement and animosity. The solid E causes them to go towards the world and mingle seriously with their prey while the solid N instinct enables them to quickly figure out how to imitate their prey (grin, recognize what words with passionate significance to the state, and so forth). There is banter in writing about whether the insane people group on J (left mind) or P(right cerebrum) side or whether it's nevertheless a continuum of psychopathy. In all probability, it's a continuum with various specialization of work among predators. They share no different qualities aside from ENTJ being carelessly objective-driven in any case the human cost (the domineering jerk) while the ENTP is disarranged yet better ready to imitate/coexist with various people and innovatively misuse that capacity (the Con Artist). Their absence of enthusiastic knowledge and want for exploitative alternate ways makes them poor technocrats, unskilled workers, and cutting edge experts. The subclinical ones could be guided the correct way and made beneficial individuals from the network. They have extra "issue" portrayals of hypomania and narcissism.

Schizotypal Personality Disorder

Almost certain among INTPs and INFPs - The key component is by all accounts a very high P that can make a flood of insightful information making a pseudo-mental trip impact. An N of 100 and a P of 100 can without much of a stretch make paranoid fears that aren't there.

Marginal Personality Disorder

More probable among ESTPs - These exhausted deadpan individuals (high P and T) live on the edge and, in this manner, make great troopers or crooks. They don't have the instinct to be insane people and don't cooperate with such a large number of different individuals as frequently since they won't get along. A very high E is critical and makes them look for seeking after amusement in the present time and place (S) that would be overpowering to most.

CHAPTER ONE

WHAT YOU NEED TO KNOW ABOUT PSYCHOLOGICAL DISORDERS

The mental issue is otherwise called a mental issue. They are mind anomalies bringing about relentless standards of conduct that can influence the everyday functionalities and life by and large. The clutters are various, and they can incorporate temperament issues, insane issues, a character issue, dietary issues, and sexual issues among numerous others. They can be harming a result of their belongings, and there is constantly a need to look for therapeutic help to keep matters in charge.

The Causes

The particular reasons for these scatter are not clear. Be that as it may, there are various elements accepted to enormously add to their event. They incorporate heredity, pre-birth exposures, concoction irregular characteristics, youth encounters, stress, and sicknesses. A portion of these scatters will, in general, be progressively regular in ladies, and others appear to be normal in men. For example, discouragement and marginal character progressively visit in ladies while substance misuse and discontinuous hazardous issue are increasingly normal in men. Schizophrenia and bipolar issues then again influence the two people similarly.

The Symptoms

The mental issue can have differing indications; however, for the most part, the social and temperament side effects are normal. The indications can be backsliding or incessant meddling with appropriate society connections. A portion of the disarranges can likewise accompany physical indications. The most widely recognized indications of the disarranges are:

- Anxiety
- Social withdrawal

- Problem disavowal

- Drug misuse and liquor misuse

- Energy level modifications

- Disconnectedness and perplexity

- Mood changes and fractiousness

- Erratic conduct, mental trips, and even daydreams

- Physical manifestations like hunger and weight changes rest unsettling influences, laziness and puzzling physical issues

Whenever left untreated, the side effects can get extreme in that the enduring individual can wind up creating self-destructive practices, undermining, injury, and powerlessness to deal with himself and his fundamental needs. It is imperative to look for treatment when the side effects appear.

The Treatment

The mental issue, simply like the most different issue, can be dealt with the correct treatment. The treatment offered will be reliant on the particular issue you are experiencing and the manifestations you have. Your PCP will be in a situation to assess the circumstance and prescribe the correct medicines or drugs to assist you with getting over the circumstance. The most well-known medicines accessible incorporate the utilization of hostile to nervousness meds and antidepressants to help improve the mind-sets. Antipsychotic drugs can likewise be utilized to treat thought designs that are cluttered and recognitions that are modified. Psychological, social treatment is additionally a decent treatment for the clutters to take a shot at the conduct and thought designs. Still, on treatment, family treatment is utilized to build up some understanding and backing for the enduring people. Gathering treatments help in ensuring that the patient doesn't wind up feeling like he is enduring alone. The individual can discover support from different patients as they progress in the direction of recuperation. Bolster treatments work extraordinary for the vast majority, and this is likewise a treatment procedure numerous specialists will set up since it keeps future events of the disarranges under control which is generally useful. There are a few distinct kinds of mental issues that influence a huge number of individuals regular. A confusion can influence anybody and can be expedited by any number of things that can occur in one's life. The sort of turmoil is typically dictated by the underlying driver and furthermore the side effects that an individual is encountering alongside any family medicinal history of mental issues. In this piece, you will find out about a few, yet not the entirety of the kinds of the mental issue alongside the normal manifestations. A nervousness issue is one kind of confusion that is related to an unsavory and overpowering mental strain or stresses that have no clear reason. These stresses can cause a fit of anxiety in certain individuals that experience the ill effects of nervousness issues. Individuals that have a tension issue have manifestations that can incorporate stressing too much, worries about a circumstance that prompts unreasonable feelings of dread, and dread of future fits of anxiety. Individuals with this sort of mental issue experience difficulty dozing and can all of a sudden loss or put on weight as their dietary patterns change. At the point when a fit of anxiety happens, you can encounter insecurity, discombobulation and the inclination that you may blackout. Additionally, deadness and shivering alongside a quick pulse, perspiring and cold, moist hands are manifestations of a nervousness assault. Presumably, one of the most widely recognized issues is misery. Eventually, everybody feels miserable or discouraged; however, an individual that can not leave their discouraged state inside two or three weeks might be experiencing despondency. A few manifestations of misery can be an observable change in dietary patterns, loss of delight from things that you regularly appreciate and lost vitality. With this kind of mental issue, one can feel a sentiment of misery and uselessness. Hesitation and the powerlessness to think can be manifestations of discouragement. Different kinds of disarranges are Childhood Disorders, Bipolar Disorders, Eating Disorders, and Post Traumatic Stress Disorder (PTSD). These mental issues have various indications to search for, yet a portion of the manifestations are like those related to misery. There are a few different kinds of disarranges, other than the ones that are referenced in this article. On the off chance that you experience or know anybody that has encountered any indications of a mental issue, counseling a specialist is significant. Any adjustment in conduct, dietary patterns, dozing designs, work execution, or social examples can be cautioning signs that should be tended to. The previous confusion is identified and treated, the simpler it will be to continue an ordinary way of life. Deciding whether somebody to be sure has a mental issue can be troublesome, and it now and again can be ignored. Since sadness manifestations are like the side effects of a few other mental issue, numerous individuals imagine that it is only a stage or feeling that will leave alone. Curiously, doctors will now and again miss analyzing a mental issue as either a physical issue or a therapeutic sickness on account of the side effect similitudes. That is the reason it is imperative to counsel with your PCP and be totally legitimate in responding to the specialists' questions.

Numerous clinicians have been attempting to portray mental illnesses, in the light of their sign. The greater part of the occasions, they like to utilize dream translation so as to show signs of improvement clarification of why the illness shows up and how it tends to be halted or oversaw. One of every seven to ten individuals living in America will require therapeutic assistance for the mental issue once in their lives. Knowing about these scatters better gets ready for individuals to manage circumstances when they happen. How about we comprehend what precisely is Abnormal Psychology Disorders? Strange practices can raise a great deal of ruckus to an individual and harm their condition. It is said that the human mind has a ton of savage and wild perspectives. Carl Jung has done broad research in this field, moreover. At the point when we see irregular practices, we attempt to get them, and we are likewise attempting to make sense of approaches to evacuate the reason for the issues. However, we before long begin to understand that the cognizant personality is attacked by peculiar sensations, thoughts and sentiments. This is the means by which an individual gets forceful. The primary indications of strange conduct are doubt and dread. The psychotic patients will, in general, fear others.

Strange Psychology Symptoms

Doubt

Dread

Nervousness Disorders

Dissociative Disorders

Somatoform Disorders and Factitious Disorders

Mind-set Disorders

Suicide

Mental Factors

Character Disorders

Drive Control Disorders

Substance-Related Disorders

Sexual Dysfunctions and Disorders

Psychological Disorders

Disarranges of Childhood and Adolescence

Mental Retardation,

Dietary issues

Irregular Psychology Help

The way to deal with assistance Abnormal Psychology Disorder patients can be through three points of view. Numerous clinician utilizes one or numerous y points of view to comprehend and treat such patients.

Social: This methodology utilizes discernible practices to comprehend irregular brain science. The therapist will concentrate on building positive conduct in understanding.

Therapeutic: In this methodology, the analyst will utilize a medicinal way to deal with comprehend and discover the main driver of organic causes and their impact on emotional well-being. The objective here for the clinician is to discover basic reasons for the anomalous issue. Prescription is fundamentally utilized for treating patients. Likewise, some other social treatment is utilized alongside medicinal assistance. Intellectual: Another methodology is to see how inner contemplations, discernments influence mental issues. This methodology is called subjective methodology. The exertion on some portion of the therapist is to change how a patient's inner idea example and response process. This is done through a procedure known as a psychological, social treatment.

Misdiagnosis of Psychological Disorders

Medicinal blunder alludes to preventable negative impacts of care or treatment that could hurt the patient. A therapeutic mistake can appear as off base analyses, careless treatment of sickness, individual damage, bacterial contamination, or different kinds of conditions. On the off chance that a specialist neglects to analyze a patient's condition or doesn't recognize the condition in an auspicious way, the patient could endure unnecessarily. The mental issue can be pulverizing for patients to suffer without the best possible treatment. On the off chance that you presume that restorative carelessness or misdiagnosis caused you mischief or damage, talk with a learned lawyer today about your case. You could be qualified to get remuneration for the harms that you have caused.

Kinds of Misdiagnosed Psychological Disorders

Numerous kinds of conditions require a quick and auspicious determination with the goal that the patient starts treatment as quickly as time permits. On the off chance that the patient's condition isn't immediately distinguished, the person could endure wounds or an extreme declining of the condition. Regular sorts of misdiagnosed mental conditions include:

- Schizophrenia

- Bipolar issue

- Major despondency

- Adult ADHD

- Alzheimer Disease

- Epilepsy

Conditions, for example, the bipolar issue, could be mixed up with significant melancholy. There could likewise belong deferrals in diagnosing a condition like schizophrenia. Mental ailments can be exceptionally incapacitating for patients and their families. Getting auspicious findings and treatment can improve things significantly in a patient's personal satisfaction. Talk with a lawyer today on the off chance that you trust you have been the casualty of a misdiagnosed state of a mental sort. You might be qualified to look for remuneration under the law.

Mental Disorder and Illnesses

The capricious issue is a remarkable mental condition in those patients present with surrounded side effects of non-peculiar fancies, however with the nonattendance of unmistakable mind flights and no accepted issue, state of mind condition, or considerable smoothing of effect. For that determination to be made, sound-related just as obvious mind flights can't be outstanding, however olfactory or responsive pipedreams related with the data from the dream might be existing. To be recognized as having a fanciful issue, the genuine dream or hallucinations can't be a direct result of the consequences of medicine, prescription, or even normal ailment, and the capricious issue can't be analyzed inside an individual once in the past determined to have schizophrenia. An individual with the silly issue may be high working in your ordinary living since this condition has no connection to an individual's IQ, and couldn't display odd or even odd conduct beside these sorts of fancies. The capricious issue is normally found in individuals who experience the ill effects of odd schizophrenia, peculiar character condition, and any extra strange issue. The genuine DSM-IV, just as analysts, by and large, concur that individual convictions ought to be assessed with superb respect so as to multifaceted design related with social just as otherworldly contrasts in light of the fact that a couple of societies have extensively perceived convictions which might be viewed as hallucinating inside different ethnicities.

The War Within

Schizophrenia is a mental issue portrayed by a breakdown related to musings by poor passionate responsiveness. Run of the mill indications incorporate oral mental trips, odd or even odd dreams, or even chaotic talk and considering, which is joined by noteworthy social or even business-related brokenness. The beginning of signs and side effects ordinarily happens in youthful adulthood, having an overall lifetime commonness of around 7 %. The analysis depends on watched conduct, and the patients accounted for encounters. Hereditary qualities, early air, neurobiology, and mental and friendly strategies appear to be significant contributory variables; some relaxation just as physician endorsed drugs seem to trigger or even exacerbate side effects. Current logical examinations are centered around the job related to neurobiology, in spite of the fact that not one segregated natural trigger has been found. The numerous potential mixes of signs and side effects have achieved on banter if the guess speaks to a solitary condition or an amount of under the radar disorders. Notwithstanding the historical underpinnings from the term from the Ancient Greek roots skein "to part" and phren, phren-("mind"), schizophrenia doesn't mean the "split character," or even "various character issue" (that is perceived nowadays in light of the fact that dissociative recognizable proof issue)- a condition that it is typically confounded in broad daylight places recognition. Rather, the word shows the "parting related to mental capacities" because of the symptomatic introduction from the sickness. The genuine column related to treatment strategies is antipsychotic prescription, which fundamentally represses dopamine (and regularly serotonin) receptor work out. Psychotherapy, just as expert and friendly restoration, will likewise be significant in treatment. In extra genuine situations where there's a threat to self just as others-automatic an emergency clinic stay might be required, albeit restorative focus remains are currently shorter and less regular than they were before, as per Psychiatrists.

The genuine condition is thought basically so as to influence cognizance, however it likewise by and large add to constant issues with a lead just as feeling. People with schizophrenia are probably going to have extra (comorbid) conditions, for example, burdensome issue and tension issue; the genuine lifetime event related to substance misuse is practically half. Agreeable issues, for instance, long haul joblessness, lower salary, and vagrancy, are commonplace. The regular life expectancy of individuals with the condition is Twelve to 15 years not as much as people without, brought about by raised physical medical problems alongside a higher suicide rate (about 5%).

The Fear of Fear Itself

Abnormal character condition is actually a state of mind seen as a dread alongside an unavoidable, long-standing suspiciousness and summed up doubt of others. Individuals with this character issue may be easily affected, easily feel insulted, and routinely associate with the planet through careful filtering of the environment as to insights or even suggestions that may check their very own apprehensions or even attitudes. Suspicious people are sharp spectators. They think they are in peril and search for signs just as dangers of that risk, possibly not so much acknowledging other verification.

The fit of anxiety Disorder

There is numerous mental issue out there that can influence individuals in a significant manner. The most mental issue is aimless; it can influence nearly anybody: men, ladies, the old, and even youngsters. Albeit some mental issue, for example, fit of anxiety issue and summed up uneasiness issue, really fall under the classification tension issue, there is one thing in the same way as a mental issue, however, all sufferers will unquestionably confront significant difficulties in their everyday lives. People who are lucky enough to not have such mental issue will ideally locate that understanding these psychological sicknesses can assist them with showing signs of improvement valuation for what sufferers are experiencing each day. One specific mental issue that is more typical than a great many people believe is a confusion called Generalized Anxiety Disorder, also called GAD. Summed up nervousness issue is, practically, simple, wouldn't you say? People who experience the ill effects of this condition can show indications of dread from an assortment of circumstances, protests, or considerably others. As the name proposes, the sufferer's dread is summed up, which means they could fear an alternate number of things. Manifestations of such type of confusion can incorporate muscle strain, trouble dozing, weariness, peevishness, and trouble focusing or concentrating on a specific errand. The referenced side effects alone will make you consider what it must want to awaken each day with this condition. For the condition to be analyzed as confusion, the side effects must keep on showing for over a half year. The side effects ought to be not kidding enough that it is meddling with the sufferer's everyday life. The treatment for this kind of condition can differ from hostile to uneasiness drugs to treatment, which shows the sufferer how to manage worry so as to get a grip on the signs. Schizophrenia is another genuine mental ailment that, regardless of its critical increase in fame through the media, not many individuals truly comprehend. There is a wide range of indications with regard to schizophrenia. Be that as it may, among the most fundamental of indications may incorporate suspicion, visualizations, hearing voices, and hallucinations. Treatment for this sort of state of mind requires an everyday portion of antipsychotics, which must be recommended by a therapist. Individuals who are schizophrenic must remain on their prescription; generally, the side effects will just deteriorate. Untreated schizophrenia can prompt the sufferer being totally lost inside their own world. Being separated from reality can have genuine outcomes. Albeit genuinely unprecedented, a few schizophrenics can become rough whenever left untreated. Tension issue, once in a while known as fit of anxiety issue, is a mental condition that is very regular among teenagers and full developed grown-ups. People who have this kind of condition experience the ill effects of incessant fits of anxiety. This type of turmoil can effectively affect a person's everyday life since the condition can be very incapacitating. The assaults are generally brought about by nerves that the individual may have for quite a while. The vast majority of us may have encountered a fit of anxiety more than once in our lives, yet individuals with a genuine issue will encounter alarm assaults all the more habitually, once in a while three to four times each week. The recurrence alone is sufficient to disturb the lifestyle of any person.

Anorexia - A Psychological Disorder, Not Just a Weight Problem

Anorexia has consistently been arranged overwhelmingly as a weight issue, and numerous individuals, particularly young people, will, in general, escape everyone's notice when seen in this light. As it were, except if you were beneath a specific weight, you were not liable to be determined to have Anorexia Nervosa. The new order in the DSM-V (indicative Statistical Manual of Mental Disorders) has expelled this attention on weight by and large and advances a comprehension of the confusion as a mental one. The new characterization, basically, helps with getting the dietary issue before the patient turns out to be hazardously slim by consolidating distinctive weight reaches and focussing consideration on mental practices related to weight reduction. By moving concentration to unfortunate associations with nourishment, utilizing diet pills or intestinal medicines, and extraordinary practicing or 'cleansing' practices, we will be unquestionably bound to get young people and others with a dietary issue in the beginning periods. The advantages of this are self-evident; getting anorexia before there has been a gigantic weight reduction brings about a greatly improved guess and enables the patient to be treated in an outpatient setting. Understanding the new criteria implies that more consideration should be paid to the obsessive practices that encompass dietary problems and understanding that these clutters, particularly anorexia, are not just about being excessively dainty. Truth be told, overweight and corpulent patients risk having this issue when they attempt to lose their weight in an undesirable manner. So we have to pay special mind to all body types and weight ranges while watching out for the mental association with nourishment and the obsessive practices that accompany weight increase or misfortune. At the point when a youngster in the ordinary weight territory starts to lose a lot of weight, individuals become concerned. In any case, when an overweight or large young person loses masses of weight, he/she is complimented. Nobody stops to ask exactly how this individual figured out how to lose the weight they did, and imagine a scenario where that weight reduction doesn't stop there. That equivalent young person might just keep on getting thinner until they are never again solid and by this stage, it will have been past the point of no return. In the event that consideration was paid to the practices related with the weight reduction, for example, regardless of whether diet pills or intestinal medicines were being utilized, or whether there was cleansing conduct, maybe a dietary issue would have been analyzed before and kept this young person from battling with a genuine mental issue.

The new basis in the DSM-V replaces the weight measure with one that peruses: "Confinement of vitality consumption comparative with prerequisites, prompting an essentially low body weight with regards to age, sex, formative direction, and physical wellbeing.

Fundamentally low weight is characterized as a weight that is not exactly insignificantly typical or, for kids and teenagers, not exactly negligibly anticipated." Furthermore, the DSM-V additionally replaces the dread of weight gain rule with "relentless conduct that meddles with weight gain" and ultimately has evacuated the measure of having at any rate 3 missed menses inside and out. Anorexia is named mellow, moderate, or extremely dependent on BMI, and there is likewise the expansion of "going away" to represent future eating practices that don't completely meet the criteria for anorexia. These new criteria move the concentration to neurotic conduct and frames of mind towards weight and permit a more extensive comprehension of the turmoil as more than simply a weight issue.

CHAPTER TWO

COGNITIVE BEHAVIORAL THERAPY

Intellectual Behavioral treatment (CBT) is a successive kind of talk treatment (psychotherapy). You work with a psychological well-being advocate (psychotherapist or advisor) in an organized way, going to a confined assortment of sessions. CBT can assist you with knowing negative or wrong reasoning, so you may see testing circumstances all the more unmistakably and respond to them in a superior way. CBT can be an amazingly helpful apparatus - either autonomously or related to different medications - in relieving psychological wellness issues, similar to sorrow, post-horrendous nervousness issues (PTSD), or a dietary issue. In any case, not every person who gains from CBT incorporates an emotional well-being condition. CBT can be an incredible instrument to assist anybody with seeing how to all the more likely handle upsetting life conditions.

Why it is finished

Subjective Behavioral treatment is utilized to manage a huge grouping of issues. It is regularly the favored sort of psychotherapy since it can assist you with distinguishing and manage specific difficulties. It ordinarily includes fewer sessions than different sorts of treatment and should be possible in an organized way.

CBT is a Useful apparatus to manage passionate difficulties. By Way of Example, it can help you:

•   Handle indications of psychological maladjustment

•   Avoid the risk of psychological maladjustment indications

•   Heal a mental disease when prescriptions are not a Fantastic other option

•   Learn techniques for managing unpleasant life circumstances

- Identify techniques to deal with emotions

- Resolve relationship battles and discover better approaches to pass on

- Deal with anguish or misfortune

- Conquer mental injury related to misuse or savagery

- Cope with a medicinal sickness

- Manage interminable physical side effects

Enthusiastic Wellbeing Ailments which could improve with CBT contain:

1. Depression

2. Anxiety issue

3. Phobias

4. PTSD

5. Sleep issue

6. Eating issue

7. Obsessive-habitual issue (OCD)

8. Substance use issue

9. Kidney afflictions

10. Schizophrenia

11.   Sexual afflictions

In specific Instances, CBT is viable when it is joined with different treatments, similar to antidepressants or different medications.

Perils

In General, there is next to no peril in getting intellectual conduct treatment. In any case, you may feel genuinely awkward periodically. This is simply because CBT can allow you to investigate incapacitating sentiments, feelings, and undertakings. You may yell, blow up, or feel distraught during a session that is intense. You could likewise feel depleted. A few Types of CBT, for example, introduction treatment, may ask that you face circumstances you would prefer to maintain a strategic distance from - like planes in the event that you have a dread of flying. This may bring about brief pressure or anxiety. Be that as it may, Working with a talented specialist may limit any dangers. The working aptitudes you learn will assist you in taking care of and overcome negative feelings and nerves.

The manner in which you plan

You may choose your own you wish to endeavor subjective conduct treatment. Or then again, a doctor or another person may show treatment to you. Here is the best approach to start: Find an advisor. It's conceivable to discover a referral by a doctor, medical coverage program, companion, or other confided in source. Numerous organizations give directing referrals or administrations through worker help programs (EAPs). Or then again, it is conceivable to find an advisor in your - for instance, through a state or nearby mental affiliation or via looking through the net.

Know the costs. At the point when you have medical coverage, realize what strategy it accommodates psychotherapy. Some wellbeing programs spread only a specific number of treatment sessions every year. Also, talk with your advisor about charges and installment decisions.

Review your very own interests. Before your first arrangement, consider what issues you need to take a shot at. Despite the fact that you may likewise type this out with your specialist, with some vibe in advance may offer a starting point.

Check certifications

Psychotherapist Is a general term rather than a task name or indication of tutoring, preparing, or licensure. Instances of psychotherapists incorporate specialists, clinicians, authorized proficient mentors, authorized social laborers, authorized marriage and family advisors, mental medical caretakers, or other certified experts with psychological well-being guidance.

Prior to Seeing a psychotherapist, survey their

Backdrop and tutoring. Prepared psychotherapists may have various distinctive occupation titles, in view of their training and capacity. Most have an ace's or doctoral certificate with unique preparing in enthusiastic guiding. Therapeutic specialists who spend significant time in psychological wellness (therapists) can recommend medicates notwithstanding give psychotherapy. Affirmation and accreditation. Guarantee the advisor you select meets state authorizing and affirmation prerequisites for their particular control. The locale of skill. Inquire as to whether the specialist has understanding and experience treating your manifestations or your fields of concern, such as dietary problems or PTSD. The key is to find a gifted specialist that will coordinate the structure and power of treatment with your prerequisites. All that you can foresee Intellectual Behavioral treatment could be performed 33% or in the two gatherings with family unit or with the individuals who have comparable issues. Online assets can be discovered, which may make taking part in CBT potential, especially if you dwell in a spot with hardly any neighborhood emotional well-being sources. CBT much of the time Contains:

1.   Learning about your mental wellbeing state

2.   Learning and rehearsing strategies like solace, adapting, perseverance, stress the executives and confidence

Your underlying treatment session

In your first semester, your specialist may regularly assemble data about you and ask what addresses you need to work on. The specialist will likely get some information about your present and past physical and mental wellbeing to acquire a more profound cognizance of your own circumstance. Your specialist can examine whether you may profit by extra treatment as well, similar to drugs. The main Session is additionally an open door for you to meet your advisor to see if he or she'll be a phenomenal fit for you. Guarantee you know:

•   Her or His procedure

•   What Sort of treatment is Suitable for you by

and by

- The points of your treatment

- The span of every session

- Exactly what number of treatment sessions you will require It may simply take a few sessions to your specialist to totally appreciate your interests and circumstance, and furthermore to determine the most reasonable strategy. On the off chance that you don't feel great with the principal specialist, you visit, attempt another person. Utilizing a good"match" together with your specialist can assist you with getting the most extreme profit by CBT.

All through CBT

Your Therapist will rouse you to talk about your own thoughts and emotions and what is troubling you. Try not to be concerned in the event that you think that it's intense to fire up about your own sentiments. Your specialist can assist you with increasing more certainty and unwinding. CBT Generally centers around specific issues, utilizing an objective situated system. As you continue all through the treatment system, your specialist may request that you perform assignments - activities, practices, or perusing, which expand on what you realize in your typical treatment sessions - and welcome you to apply what you realize in your standard life. Your Therapist's system will be reliant on your particular circumstance and tastes. Your advisor can consolidate CBT with an alternate restorative methodology - for example, relational treatment, which moves in your associations with various people.

Measures in CBT

CBT Typically contains these measures:

1.   Identify upsetting situations or conditions in your lifetime. These might incorporate such issues as a wellbeing condition, separate, misery, outrage, or indications of a psychological wellness condition. You and your advisor can invest energy figuring out what issues and objectives that you have to focus on.

2.   Become aware of your considerations, convictions, and sentiments about these issues. When

you've recognized the issues to take a shot at, your specialist may propel you to talk about your thoughts regarding them. This may incorporate seeing what you educate yourself about an undertaking (self-talk), your own translation of the noteworthiness of a situation, and your convictions about yourself, others, and events. Your advisor may suggest that you keep a diary of your thoughts.

3.   Identify incorrect or negative reasoning. That will assist you with understanding examples of reasoning and conduct which may be adding to an issue; your specialist may request that you take a gander at your physical, mental, and social responses in different situations.

4.   Reshape incorrect or negative reasoning. Your advisor will presumably inspire you to ask if your point of view of a situation depends on the real world or on a mistaken comprehension of what's going on. This measure can be testing. You may have long-standing strategies for considering your own life and yourself. With work out, valuable reasoning and personal

conduct standards will turn into a propensity and won't take as a lot of work.

Length of treatment

CBT is Generally viewed as momentary treatment - going from roughly five to 20 sessions. You and your advisor may talk about what number of sessions could be ideal for you. Perspectives to consider include:

- Sort of ailment or situation

- Severity your indications

- How long you have encountered your indications or happen to adapt to your conditions

- How quick you make progress

- Just how much pressure you are encountering

- Just how much help You Get from family just as others

Classification

Aside from Very explicit conditions, talks with your advisor are classified. Be that as it may, an advisor can break secrecy if there's a quick risk of security or whenever required by administrative or state law to report issues to the government. These situations include:

1.   Threatening to right away or in a matter of seconds (inescapably) hurt yourself or end your life

2.   Threatening to quickly damage or end the Life Span of another person

3.   Abusing a youngster or a defenseless grown-up - someone over age 18 who is hospitalized or left open to an impairment

4.   Being unfit to securely treat for yourself

5.   Outcomes

6.   Cognitive Behavioral treatment probably won't fix your ailment or make a horrendous circumstance leave. In any case, it might give you the capacity to deal with your circumstance in a sound way and to rest easy thinking about your very own life.

Getting the most extreme from CBT

CBT isn't effective for everyone. Be that as it may, you can make a move to get irrefutably the most from your treatment and make it a triumph.

1.   Strategy treatment for an association. Treatment is best once you're a functioning player and talk about it in the end. Be sure you and your specialist concur concerning the critical issues and how to deal with them. Together, you may set targets and assess progress after some time.

2.   Be legitimate and open. Accomplishment with treatment is reliant upon your eagerness to discuss your thoughts, feelings, and emotions, and on being open to new bits of knowledge and strategies for getting things done. In the event that you are hesitant to talk about specific things because of crippling emotions, mortification, or tensions about your specialist's reaction, let your advisor think about your appointments.

3.   Stick to a treatment technique. Should you're feeling down or need inspiration, at that point, it could

be enticing to sidestep treatment sessions. Doing this can intrude on your advancement. Go to all sessions and give some plan to what you wish to go over.

4.   Do not anticipate quick outcomes. Taking a shot at mental issues can be crippling, and habitually requires difficult work. It isn't irregular to feel more terrible during the main segment of treatment as you begin to look at various times clashes. You may require a few sessions until you begin to see improvement.

5.   Do your assignments between sessions. On the off chance that your advisor requests that you read, keep up a diary, or perform different undertakings outside your ordinary treatment sessions, at that point track. Doing such schoolwork assignments can enable you to apply what you've heard in the treatment sessions.

6.   If treatment isn't talking, with your advisor. On the off chance that you don't accept you're benefitting from CBT after a couple of sessions, at that point, talk with your specialist about it. You and your specialist may decide to create a few changes or attempt

another methodology.

Intellectual Behavioral Therapy (CBT) is a system that tends to broken sentiments conduct, and psychological methodology dependent on a composite of essential subjective and social standards and procedures. CBT is issue centered and activity arranged methodology advisors use to assist patients with tending to specific issues like melancholy, nervousness, and substantially more convoluted mental issues. Subjective Behavioral Therapy distinguishes various organized methodology of psychotherapy that inside on the musings supporting a patient's issues. 1 survey of right around 2,300 analysts from the USA found that approximately 70 percent use CBT related to different medications to treat melancholy and stress. CBT is likewise an overwhelming psychotherapy worldview now being taught in brain research graduate-level applications.

How Cognitive Behavior Therapy Works
Subjective Behavioral Therapy depends on the thought that individuals are nonsensical and win a decent

arrangement of strange blunders each time they assess the dangers and focal points of different conditions and classes of the thoughts and activities. This may result in crazy feelings like wretchedness and outrage. In any case, CBT can likewise be used to manage an assortment increasingly confounded issues, for instance, Post-horrendous Anxiety Disorder (PTSD), OCD, substance misuse, ADHD, dietary issues, bipolar malady, among the different issue. Psychological Behavioral Therapists must have an awesome association with their patients to this to succeed, for example, extraordinary relational abilities and a fabulous fit in character types. This is on the grounds that specialists and patients work together to discuss the current issues alongside the patient's accepting thoughts for her or his thoughts and activities towards these troubles. The best reason for existing is to change figuring designs so the individual may experience less constantly negative mental states. The National Alliance for Mental Health for CBT since it's magnificent logical data supporting its utilization in the clinical treatment of mental disease, and it's accomplished wide fame both for the two patients and competitors the same. An expanding number of analysts, therapists, social specialists, and mental medical caretakers have to prepare in CBT. Research On the adequacy of CBT has been appeared to work for an expansive assortment of illnesses. These investigations are well-controlled, the information has been analyzed acceptably, and the outcomes represent themselves. By method, for example, CBT has been demonstrated to give generous advantages in getting a bipolar issue and driving fewer days in the emergency clinic, decreased degrees of suicide, and diminished degrees of para-self-destructive or self-damaging conduct.

Safety measures To Consider Before Beginning Cognitive Behavior Therapy

Therapists, Clinical analysts, social specialists, and other emotional wellness experts finish long stretches of instruction and preparing, yet it's conceivable to rehearse treatment with this a decent preparing foundation. A few things to think about before settling upon a CBT proficient are the instructive foundation and preparing, and some other authority affiliations do they have a place, like the Association for Behavioral and Cognitive Therapies, where many driving specialists are partners.

Before visiting a creation your underlying arrangement, evaluate their history, instruction, confirmation, and affirmation. A psychotherapist is every now and again used as a general term. Guarantee the advisor you select meets state permitting and accreditation necessities for their particular order. The mystery is to get a gifted advisor that will coordinate the structure and treatment with your prerequisites. Commonly, CBT is compelling when it's joined with different treatments, such as ingesting medications. In this way, just as a specialist, you may likewise require a clinician for endorsing drugs. Something else to consider is the cost. On the off chance that you have medicinal protection, realize what strategy it accommodates your treatment sessions. Some wellbeing programs spread only a specific number of treatment sessions every year. Some probably won't be managed in any capacity. Along these lines, make sure to address the advisor in regard to charges and installment alternatives before your underlying outing.

Outline

Prior to Your underlying interview, consider what issues you're having that require treatment. In spite of the fact that you may likewise sift through some of this with your own advisor, gaining a phenomenal feeling of your issues in advance will help as a beginning stage. Once more, check to their certifications and experience, particularly with your very own issues. A few advisors probably won't satisfy the capabilities you need. In the event that you don't locate the ideal one the first run through the round, don't quit attempting. Get your work done, and you'll be able to find an incredible Cognitive Behavioral Therapist.

Subjective conduct treatment was used to help

patients that experience the ill effects of melancholy, nerves, addictions, and a wide range of other psychosocial issues. When Undergoing psychological conduct treatment, an expert helps the tormented individual to correct their reasoning. It's an idea that reasoning examples and how an individual could see or connection to explicit circumstances are connected with the person's feelings and conduct. Subjective Behavior treatment is a way to help locate the hidden reasons for the issue from a mental viewpoint and change or modify the reasoning example, which has brought about wrong conduct. Using Cognitive conduct treatment, a specialist is endeavoring to adjust the twisted thinking about this person. This thusly will help the person to make changes in conduct and to be able to re-alter. Thinking examples and feelings assume an essential job in human conduct and might be adjusted or changed. Psychological Behavior treatment can be used to help individuals with medicating reliance like cocaine. In the strictest feeling of the term, individuals who go to drugs, both lawful physician endorsed drugs that are addictive, notwithstanding illicit medications, are thought to have a conduct issue and may profit by psychological conduct treatment. You will locate A developing measure of people that experience the ill effects of broken sicknesses and keeping in mind that others figure therapeutic cures could be adequate. Studies seem to infer that intellectual conduct treatment is fruitful. Clearly, a ton relies on the person's readiness to comply with a prepared advisor and furthermore to change inner considerations and sentiments. The Trained specialist additionally encourages the person to comprehend past experiences and situations, to analyze, and to figure out how to not react in a crazy or reshaped way. Psychological Behavior treatment is currently a technique for understanding the connection between inside thoughts and faculties and human conduct. This no uncertainty has prompted a triumph that has been made. Also, it has helped a few people to make tremendous changes in their lifetime. Should you Are somebody who's encountering sorrow or tension or another kind of psycho-social trouble, take guts and distinguish a prepared specialist in intellectual conduct treatment. It is conceivable to figure out how to make changes in your very own life and help your self and individuals that are close to you. Clearly, it may require some investment to see that a distinction in your lifetime, yet remember to accomplish anything beneficial, you will require a choice. You will see as an excessive number of books expounded on this theme; you may decide to try out. While going on the web, you may likewise discover a great deal of data which may enable you to get familiar with intellectual conduct treatment. The Moment you could spend can have the effect. Interestingly, even on the occasion that you're feeling disappointed and overpowered now and again, there's assistance for you. There's likewise help in sort of workshops which you could take care of discover progressively about intellectual conduct treatment and how it can help you. Setting aside the effort to examine the data promptly accessible could be the absolute initial step for mending.

In what manner can This Procedure Function?

Intellectual Behavioral treatment is a talking strategy or treatment for an assortment of sorts of issues like resting and eating malady, nervousness issues, useless feelings, prescription maltreatment, conduct issue, a character issue, and mind-set issues. CBT utilizes frameworks and strategies as an approach to different sorts of conduct and mental issue. There are a ton of strategies utilized for this treatment; for instance, normal conduct treatment, logic conduct treatment, reasonable living treatment, judicious emotive conduct treatment, and subjective treatment. CBT is a two-route exchange since the individual should express her thoughts and emotions, while the advisor listens to mentors and empowers the person.

The Cognitive Model of enthusiastic reaction that is subjective social treatment is an incredible one since its establishment is a person's considerations that are sufficiently able to adjust her conduct, sentiments, and viewpoint. CBT is famously alluded to like the kind of treatment that offers extraordinary advantages in a shorter timespan in contrast with different cures and cures. CBT is likewise a period restricted treatment; anyway, it's additionally a ceaseless technique. CBT permits a patient to perform treatments and errands on her when she's at home. The results of the activity or mission are talked about and explained during treatment sessions. Besides customary treatment sessions, there are loads of valuable expert and simple distributions about the intellectual, social treatment that will help somebody who's encountering mental pain. CBT has specific strategies and discernment. Every session has an alternate timetable for the program. Posing inquiries is very fundamental in each CBT session. The patient ought to solicit all from her requests and the specialists should pose the individual explicit inquiries to be able to manage a couple of issues that the patient probably won't be able to express since there are occurrences that a patient may be not able to tell precisely what she really feels. Extraordinary Approaches are heard through Cognitive, social treatment, for example, being able to adjust how individuals think and act. Figuring positive can be a piece of CBT, including counteracting and putting a conclusion to programmed negative reasoning. Another viable methodologies and techniques are hindering one's strolling and talking style. A patient likewise ought to be refreshed and refreshed as it is less complex for the treatment to sink directly into a person's brain if he's refreshed and loose. The guidance given to patients can likewise be handled easier on the off chance that somebody isn't compelled or pushed.You will discover many destinations that offer accommodating information with respect to subjective social treatment. Clarifications and models concerning CBT and the cures are likewise posted. Circumstances and circumstances are provided; loved ones of people with Psychological and social issues will get some thought of the issue, and the best approach to fix it. History of CBT and other research about it tends to be found too. In Addition, sites and articles are offered on the internet to show accommodating Information concerning this treatment. A few locales additionally give gatherings and bulletins Roughly CBT so individuals can mingle and share encounters and thoughts concerning it.

Intellectual Behavior Therapy Methods

Intellectual Behavioral treatment methods are proof-based systems to adjust sentiments, contemplations, and practices and upgrade general life fulfillment and activity. They're educated by the most recent brain science study, having shown to be perhaps the best intercession for the state of mind issue and mental issues. The psychological conduct treatment strategies recorded beneath speak to a couple of the most regular procedures in CBT, which are made to build a state of mind and conduct.

1.   Cognitive Restructuring Strategies: Cognitive rebuilding is a subjective conduct treatment system focused on helping people distinguish thinking designs responsible for harming temperaments and fruitless

conduct. There are numerous procedures used through intellectual rebuilding. The most widely recognized strategy is observing useless musings on an idea record type, and creating fitter, all the more genuinely adaptable examples of reasoning.

2.   Graded Exposure Assignments: Exposure is an intellectual conduct treatment method that helps individuals deliberately approach the things that they dread. By and large, uneasiness makes individuals avoid situations. Lamentably, the shirking of dreaded circumstances is the thing that keeps sentiments of nervousness and uneasiness. Through deliberate powerlessness, people ace feared circumstances individually, at that point, handle raising troublesome presentation missions. Presentation is among the best mental medicines, that is, gaining a 90% adequacy rate with some pressure issues.

3.   Action Assessing: Task observing is an intellectual conduct treatment method proposed to assist people with expanding practices they should accomplish more. By booking and distinguishing

helpful practices, such as pondering, going for a walking, or taking a shot at a vocation, it raises the likelihood of their getting done. This method is especially gainful for those that don't take an interest in many remunerating interests as a result of despairing , or people who experience difficulty finishing employments in light of lingering.

4.   Successive Approximation: This subjective conduct treatment strategy works for the individuals who experience difficulty completing a vocation, either as a result of the absence of commonality with this activity or as the activity appears to be overwhelming, which is as it should be. The procedure works by helping people ace a less complex errand that resembles the harder undertaking. It is practically identical to rehearsing expansion and subtraction preceding considering long division. When you're polished just as subtraction, long division isn't as overwhelming. In like manner, with practiced one conduct, one which is imperceptibly harder feels considerably more sensible.

5.   Mindfulness Exercise: Mindfulness is an intellectual conduct treatment method acquired from Buddhism. The target of care is to help people diminish ruminating or fixating on harming things and occupy their concentration on what's truly happening right now. Care is the point of loads of new examination in brain research and mirrors the outskirts of psychotherapy practice.

6.   Abilities Coaching: a lot of individuals' issues result from not getting the best possible aptitudes to understand their targets. Aptitudes guidance is an intellectual conduct treatment procedure utilized in curing such capacities deficiencies. Run of the mill places for aptitudes preparing to include social capacities preparing, imparting instructing , and decisiveness preparing. Typically aptitudes preparing happens through direct guidance, demonstrating, and pretends.

Psychological Behavioral treatment or CBT is a blend of two incredible cures: conduct and intellectual. Psychological treatment applies to the reasoning procedure and conviction framework while conduct treatment applies to individuals' exercises. The plan of CBT formed during the 1960s and can be utilized in both gathering and individual treatment settings. It had been planned and refined by different conspicuous doctors, has gotten significant analysis in the emotional wellness network, and it has endured the trial of time and negativity. Despite the fact that More customary medicines may take a long time to help an individual experiencing an illness, psychological, social treatment is reduced and require as not many as sixteen (16) sessions to decide ideal results. CBT is arranged chiefly to client targets and made to think and deal with issues a client is encountering. Psychological Behavioral treatment was found incredibly accommodating in uneasiness issue and tension issue notwithstanding schizophrenia in spite of the fact that its range is wide and manages various types of illnesses and mental issue. It generally manages the present time and place and furthermore to help accomplish the absolute best results. CBT's

Strategy is to attack the issue in earnest so as to talk and manage issues head-on. It helps invert unfavorable reasoning strategies and changes practices by modifying thinking forms. It's discovered best once a client finds the perfect reasoning activities and procedures to get themselves and actualizes them into ordinary living.

For Example, psychological conduct specialists can utilize techniques like:

1.   Teaching oneself to back off,

2.   Utilizing positive assertions or fortifications to stop negative and negative reasoning,

3.   Pay cautious regard for voices one responds to and voices which drive a person to do explicit things, and

4.   Focusing consideration on specific intentions.

In the wake of Thinking, strategies are found out, and being dealt with, conduct treatment begins. It involves executing intellectual techniques to reality and ordinary situations. Regularly it includes client"homework" assignments where the client envisions genuine situations and applies learned techniques to beat anything that is causing troubles. Additional"assignments" may comprise of rehearsing positive subjective procedures a few times every day. At the point when the mind shifts from the negative to the positive, another strategy is rehearsed and the cycle proceeds to negative reasoning and practices are no more. The most Significant favorable position of subjective conduct treatment is the way that it requires the shopper to act. The client has a progressively dynamic part in their very own treatment to manage side effects and illnesses.

An Effective Technique to Conquer Emotional Illness
A little change in our outlook can comprehend and defeat unfriendly conditions in our own life. How we act and how we react to situations to a great extent relies on our own standpoint towards life and situations that, in a roundabout way or

straightforwardly, influence our way of life. As a Psycho-remedial methodology, Cognitive Behavior Therapy encourages individuals to adopt new abilities to oversee broken practices and sentiments. This sort of treatment is used both for gatherings and people to teach them in recouping from addictions, miseries, tension assaults, stress issue, and different fears. The independent sessions in these treatment programs help in comprehension and defeating an assortment of diseases and alleviating side effects. In most of the examples, such CBT is favorable for people that experience the ill effects of different psychological well-being issues and miseries since it presents lesser risks than antidepressants just as different strategies of psychotherapies. So as To benefit the best responses for any kind of passionate infirmities through CBT, individuals ought to don't stop for a second to uncover their interests, issues, or nerves. This guides CBT masters in providing better directing and demonstrating the well-suited treatment or application for long haul benefits. They step up in understanding the ailment and its reality which may vary from individual to individual. The treatment centers around evacuating harming conduct of individuals of various age classes through precise systems. This treatment has additionally demonstrated to be a gift for those burdened by:

- Post awful pressure issue

- Insomnia

- Stress

- Eating issue

- Obsessive habitual issue

The Notion of Cognitive Behavioral Treatment created in the mid-1960s. A blend of intellectual and social treatment, CBT centers around the convictions and thoughts that help decide the manner and outlook of someone. The treatment facilitates the deduction procedure to get solid and versatile and endeavors to adjust standards of conduct that are undesirable. Any biological factors or past encounters influence one's perspective on some random situation. Much of the time, this view is curved which causes them to react to situations with a crazy response. The absolute initial phase in CBT teaches people to inspect the issue situations with supreme lucidity in order to grasp the right and appropriate reaction. CBT or Cognitive Behavioral Therapy gave by experts helps with providing total alleviation to people from conduct and mental reactions that add to upsetting situations. This treatment comes to perform when an individual intentionally examines, translates and handles his/her thoughts. As sentiments and thoughts are intertwined, people discover better authority over their feelings. Any individual who might want to control the manner of thinking can utilize this strategy and furthermore receive the most extreme rewards. CBT, though an extended strategy, is very incredible and, in this way worth the entirety of the endeavors. Consequently, it's an unfathomably well-known treatment program that helps people in Recovering from an awesome combination of sicknesses directly from melancholies to fear Disease and bulimia. In the event that You're Looking for a specific answer for your uneasiness, at that point, Ailments or miseries start searching for these CBT treatment geniuses. They could guide You in getting progressively positive throughout everyday life, keeping you from a wide range of nerves Effortlessly.

CHAPTER THREE

COGNITIVE DISORDERS

The intellectual issue is a sort of psychological well-being Disorders that principally influence memory, getting the hang of, comprehension, and critical thinking, and contain amnesia, dementia, and incoherence. The four major sorts of psychological issue are incoherence (a modification in understanding that creates inside a limited timeframe period where people have a lessened consciousness of the surroundings); dementia (an extreme weakening of cerebrum working that is set apart by hindrance of memory, perplexity, and powerlessness to think; amnesia (an increasingly significant decrease of their memory, and in spite of no absence of extra subjective capacities, for example, there's in dementia; and intellectual issue not generally indicated (subjective impedance accepted to be because of a general ailment or substance use and doesn't fit into different gatherings). The psychological issue is portrayed as any malady that significantly hinders the subjective utilization of somebody to the time when ordinary activity in the public eye is unthinkable without treatment. Some successive intellectual issue incorporates Dementia, bronchial sicknesses, Motor expertise diseases, Amnesia, Substance-initiated subjective weakness. The intellectual issue is to such an extent that inside on the mind Ability to review and process information. The reasons for the disarranges may be in essence - head injury or the degeneration of the cerebrum with maturing - anyway, they may likewise be connected to substance misuse or different causes. Markers of the psychological issue include issues with contemplating new data, notwithstanding broad issues with momentary memory and other subjective issues. In view of the exact sort of psychological infection present, the treatment decisions may differ, be that as it may, the online treatment it is conceivable to get from prepared specialists on GoMentor.com can viably help with the signs and dangers normally identified with these sorts of illnesses. Before we get to how you can get help with the remedy for subjective issues on GoMentor.com, here's a summary of the sorts of psychological issue and a couple of the signs and dangers that meet up.

Sorts of Psychological Disorders

People with intellectual issues experience the ill effects of issues that impact their ability to do at any rate one of those exercises. The intellectual issue is currently recorded as neurocognitive Ailments to demonstrate that there's some sort of interest in the psyche. The key neurocognitive issue recorded are:

<u>Wooziness:</u> A modification in accepting that creates inside a limited timeframe period and incorporates a decrease of awareness of a person's domain, circumstance, and capacity to think plainly.

Dementia: A Progressive lessening in a person's accepting that most as often as possible incorporates memory misfortune, challenges concentrating, and furthermore a decrease of extra reasoning limits.

Amnesia: Performance Reduction with no generous decrease of other reasoning aptitudes.

Others: Several different Ailments, which could be an aftereffect of ailments, utilizing the drug, and so on.

There Are Lots of other potential causes and kinds of subjective issues. It may take an entire book to record all the likely explanations of the psychological issue and, furthermore, the reasons for what's regularly known as an intellectual glitch. Intellectual brokenness is an inversion in considering the progressions that happen in psychological issue anyway is certifiably not a diagnosable illness like dementia. Some of the significant reasons for subjective issue/brokenness contain:

Qualities: Genetic Influences appear to have an impact on a few diverse psychological issues. For instance, Huntington's malady is a genuine development issue which much of the time remembers significant changes for accepting. Dementia that comes close by the malady is believed to be credited to innate causes. Alzheimer's malady is thought to have potential

80

hereditary causes in specific individuals who build up the ailment. Strokes happen when the blood supply to the mind is hindered because of blocked or stuffy corridors or veins in the cerebrum. Strokes regularly make noteworthy psychological brokenness in individuals. Strokes are believed to be the impact of a mix of hereditary variables and one's conduct like a way of life, diet, specific wellbeing conditions, and so on. A formative issue like down disorder as often as possible makes noteworthy intellectual brokenness and oftentimes are brought about by innate components.

<u>Head Injury:</u> Head Accidents can make generous intellectual glitch. They are some of the time a wellspring of afflictions, for example, dementia or amnesia. In view of the reality and degree of the head damage, the outcomes might be specific to the segment of the cerebrum that is harmed or may influence the general activity. Shut head wounds regularly make horrible cerebrum wounds (TBIs) that happen when the mind isn't entered by something.

These sorts of wounds incorporate blackouts (when the brain is shaken or ricochets from the skull), wounds into the psyche (called hematomas), alongside other comparative sorts of wounds. Somebody having horrible cerebrum damage may very well display psychological challenges associated with the area of the mind that has been influenced or may show numerous issues with speculation. Entering head wounds, such as being shot in the head, regularly just modify the district of the cerebrum that has been harmed and may or probably won't prompt general issues with intuition.

<u>Sicknesses and Diseases:</u> There Are Lots of germs, infections, and malady conditions that may affect the brain and result in subjective breakdown alongside an intellectual issue. Meningitis is an aggravation of the defensive covering of the cerebrum and spinal line which might be brought about by microbes or an infection. It might bring about the noteworthy intellectual glitch and possibly passing. Numerous scleroses (MS) is a turmoil that is thought to happen

when the body's safe framework begins to assault a compound called myelin. Myelin is a piece of the cells from the focal sensory system (the cerebrum and spinal string) which help the phones to sign to another. On the off chance that the myelin is seriously harmed, the cells can't impart, and people begin to have issues with their own reasoning and movement. Parkinson's infection happens when the phones inside the mind which make a substance called dopamine begin to bite the dust. The cells that utilization dopamine can't impart productively together. A few people with Parkinson's illness can create dementia because of these changes in the psyche. People who agreement AIDS as often as possible begin to encounter a psychological glitch. They may even create dementia because of the infection connected to AIDS.

Mind Tumors: Tumors are irregular cells that develop and infiltrate the districts of the body where they are. Tumors can be kindhearted or dangerous. Kindhearted methods they won't spread to different areas. Threatening methods that they'll spread to different areas and might keep on rising much after most of the tumor has been expelled. Tumors that happen in the psyche or in the covers of the psyche may impact the locale of the mind wherein they are . This could prompt psychological brokenness identified with that locale of the cerebrum. As an occurrence, a tumor that is at a person's location focus can affect their ability to communicate in and grasp language, yet probably won't impact different purposes. Tumors may likewise influence different districts in the psyche should they create in various locales of the psyche or should they become so huge that they begin to push up the cerebrum against the skull and furthermore impact various areas of the mind. Indeed, even activity to evacuate the tumors probably won't prompt an individual recapturing the entirety of the subjective capacities which were impacted by the tumor.

Introduction to Hazardous Compounds: There Are Lots of substances which may influence the working of this Brain and result in intellectual issue or subjective breakdown. These substances are typically known as neurotoxins. People presented to lead, or other substantial metals may make issues with their memory and other psychological capacities. Being presented to paint exhaust, the electrons out of specific sorts of pastes, bonds, gas or vaporized jars, and so on. may likewise prompt critical mind harm. This harm may bring about psychological brokenness. Utilizing liquor or medications, for example, heroin or cocaine may prompt huge subjective glitch or the development of an intellectual malady. As an occurrence, a few people who abuse liquor after some time can build up a kind of dementia in view of cerebrum harm connected to their liquor abuse. Ailing health or elective Lifestyle Factors: Not eating appropriately, getting satisfactory exercise, or different factors Related to the person's way of life may bring about the development of a psychological ailment. For instance, a condition called Wernicke Korsakoff disorder, which, as often as possible, is determined in individuals to have intense liquor addiction. That occurs because of an incredibly awful diet and not because of their liquor abuse.

Individuals who build up this illness need nutrient B1 because of a terrible eating routine. This may affect the activity of the brain and result in serious challenges with memory alongside different issues. In the event that the individual doesn't patch their eating regimen and get legitimate sustenance, the progressions can get changeless. Individuals who are overweight are likewise defenseless against a lot of exceptional sorts of subjective issues like stroke and even dementia. Extreme lack of healthy sustenance may bring about issues with incoherence.

Side effects of Psychological Disorders

The Signs of intellectual issues will differ Based on the specific kind. Anyway, they, for the most part, incorporate troubles with the cerebrum's ability to process information or recall it. Issues with momentary memory and jumbled deduction notwithstanding other physical and mental issues, are a couple of the pointers of intellectual issue. The mental issues that are because of that malady may have an extremely negative effect on various regions of a person's lifetime whenever left untreated.

1. Quick changes in mental conditions

2. Poor transient memory

3. Disorganized reasoning

4. Emotional issues - discourse, memory, understanding

5. Inability to grasp discourse

6. Learning issues

7. Memory and recall issues

8. The trouble with basic reasoning

9. Reliance on schedules and notes

Risks of Psychological Disorders

As Previously Mentioned, whenever left untreated, the intellectual issue could Quickly deteriorate, with the possibility of extra mental issues showing up. Alongside this, there would be the dangers that someone that has a psychological malady may get lost and be not ready to discover their direction home or even review what their identity is. At the point when left untreated, these sorts of diseases can get poor enough that nonstop supervision is important. Prior to it's that way, in light of the particular subjective sickness has been examined, there are bunches of various treatment alternatives accessible which could be able to give assistance.

At its essential level, the term subjective issue applies to a turmoil, malady, or condition that impedes the psychological working of the individual. This outcome in the individual's capacity to work getting incredibly troublesome or inconceivable without treatment or without some type of help. Perception is a term that alludes to:

- Different mental capacities, for example, learning and memory
- Seeing or recognizing and understanding the connections of articles in one's condition
- Tackling issues
- Getting language
- Speaking with others

- Deciding

- Having the option to consider things from various perspectives.

Individuals with the intellectual issue have issues that influence their capacity to perform at least one of these activities. As per the American Psychiatric Association's (APA) Diagnostic and Statistical Manual of Mental Disorders - Fifth Edition (DSM-5), the intellectual issue is currently recorded as a neurocognitive issue to demonstrate that there is some kind of inclusion of the mind. The principle neurocognitive issue recorded in the DSM-5 are:

Insanity: An adjustment in feeling that creates over a brief timeframe and incorporates lost attention to an individual's environment, circumstance, and capacity to think unmistakably.

Dementia: A dynamic decrease in an individual's reasoning that frequently incorporates memory misfortune, issues concentrating, and lost other reasoning capacities.

Amnesia: Memory misfortune without a huge loss of other reasoning capacities.

Others: Many different conditions that can be because of ailments, the utilization of medications, and so forth.

There are numerous other potential causes and kinds of subjective issues. It would take a whole book to list all the potential reasons for the subjective issue and the reasons for what is regularly alluded to as intellectual brokenness. Subjective brokenness is an adjustment in speculation like the progressions that occur in an intellectual issue; however, is certainly not a diagnosable issue like dementia. A portion of the significant reasons for psychological issue/brokenness include:

Qualities: Genetic impacts seem to assume a job in a wide range of intellectual issues. For example, Huntington's illness is a serious development issue that frequently remembers critical changes for the deduction. Dementia that joins the turmoil is accepted to be because of hereditary causes. Indeed, even Alzheimer's infection is accepted to have conceivable hereditary causes in certain individuals that build up the confusion. Strokes happen when the blood supply to the cerebrum is disturbed in light of burst or blocked veins or conduits in mind. Strokes regularly produce huge psychological brokenness in individuals. Strokes are accepted to be the aftereffect of a blend of hereditary elements and one's conduct, for example, diet, way of life, certain wellbeing conditions, and so forth. The formative issue, for example, Down disorder, frequently produces critical subjective brokenness and regularly is the consequence of hereditary elements.

Head Injury: Head wounds can create noteworthy subjective brokenness. They can be a wellspring of disarranges like dementia or amnesia. Contingent upon the seriousness and degree of the head damage, the impacts can be explicit to the piece of the mind that is harmed or can influence one's general working. Shut head wounds regularly produce awful mind wounds

(TBIs) that happen when the cerebrum isn't infiltrated by some item. These kinds of wounds incorporate blackouts (when the cerebrum is either shaken or ricochets against the skull), wounds to the mind (known as hematomas), and other comparable sorts of wounds. An individual with horrible mind damage may just show psychological issues related to the territory of the cerebrum that have been influenced or may show numerous issues with speculation. Entering head wounds, for example, being shot in the head, frequently just influence the zone of the mind that has been harmed and could conceivably prompt generally speaking issues with speculation.

<u>Maladies and Infections:</u> There are numerous microorganisms, infections, and sickness conditions that can influence the mind and lead to intellectual brokenness or a psychological issue. Meningitis is an irritation of the defensive covering of the cerebrum and spinal string that can be brought about by microscopic organisms or an infection. It can prompt huge intellectual brokenness and even passing.

Different sclerosis (MS) is an illness that is accepted to happen when the body's safe framework starts to assault a substance known as myelin. Myelin is a piece of the phones in the focal sensory system (the cerebrum and spinal line) that help the phones to move toward each other. At the point when the myelin is seriously harmed, the cells can't impart, and individuals start to have issues with their reasoning and development. Parkinson's illness happens when the cells in the mind that produce a concoction known as dopamine bite the dust. The cells that utilization dopamine can't discuss viably with each other. A few people with Parkinson's illness may create dementia on account of these adjustments in the cerebrum. Individuals who agreement AIDS regularly start to encounter intellectual brokenness. They may even create dementia in view of the infection-related to AIDS.

<u>Mind Tumors:</u> Tumors are irregular cells that develop and infiltrate the zones of the body where they are found. Tumors can either be considerate or

threatening. Amiable implies that they won't spread to different zones. Threatening implies that they will spread to different zones and may keep on becoming much after the majority of the tumor is evacuated. Tumors that occur in the cerebrum or in the covers of the mind can influence the region of the mind where they are found. This can bring about intellectual brokenness related to that region of the cerebrum. For instance, a tumor that is in an individual's discourse focus can influence their capacity to communicate in and get language, yet may not influence different capacities. Tumors can likewise influence different territories in the cerebrum in the event that they develop in numerous zones of the mind or on the off chance that they become so huge that they start to drive the cerebrum facing the skull and influence different zones of the mind. Indeed, even medical procedures to evacuate the tumors may not bring about an individual recapturing all the subjective capacities that were influenced by the tumor.

Introduction to Toxic Substances: There are numerous

substances that can influence the working of the mind and lead to intellectual issues or psychological brokenness. These substances are frequently alluded to as neurotoxins. Individuals presented to lead or other substantial metals can create issues with their memory and other subjective capacities. Being presented to paint exhaust, the vapor from particular kinds of pastes, bonds, fuel or airborne jars, and so forth can likewise bring about noteworthy cerebrum harm. This harm can prompt intellectual brokenness. The utilization of liquor or medications like cocaine or heroin can bring about critical intellectual brokenness or the improvement of a subjective issue. For instance, a few people who misuse liquor after some time may build up a type of dementia because of cerebrum harm identified with their liquor misuse. Lack of healthy sustenance or other Lifestyle Factors: Not eating appropriately, getting adequate exercise, or different variables related to the individual's way of life can prompt the improvement of a subjective issue. For example, a condition is known as Wernicke Korsakoff disorder that frequently is determined in individuals to have extreme liquor addiction. This happens on account of a horrible eating routine and not as a result of their liquor misuse. Individuals that build up this condition need nutrient B1 in view of a horrible eating routine. This can influence the working of the cerebrum and lead to extreme issues with memory and different issues. On the off chance that the individual doesn't fix their eating routine and get appropriate nourishment, the progressions can get perpetual. Individuals that are hefty are additionally defenseless against various kinds of a psychological issue, for example, stroke and even dementia. Extreme unhealthiness can prompt issues with insanity.

Gentle intellectual weakness (MCI) is the phase between the normal subjective decrease of ordinary maturing and the more genuine decay of dementia. It can include issues with memory, language, thinking, and judgment that are more prominent than typical age-related changes.

On the off chance that you have gentle psychological

impedance, you might know that your memory or mental capacity has "slipped." Your family and dear companions, likewise, may see a change. Yet, these progressions aren't sufficiently extreme to essentially meddle with your everyday life and regular exercises. Gentle psychological impedance may expand your danger of later creating dementia brought about by Alzheimer's illness or other neurological conditions. Be that as it may, a few people with gentle psychological weakness never deteriorate, and a couple inevitably shows signs of improvement.

Side effects

Your mind, similar to the remainder of your body, changes as you become more seasoned. Numerous individuals notice slowly expanding absent-mindedness as they age. It might take more time to think about a word or to review an individual's name. Be that as it may, predictable or expanding worry about your psychological presentation may recommend mellow intellectual weakness (MCI).

Intellectual issues may go past what's normal and show conceivable MCI on the off chance that you experience any or the entirety of the accompanying:

- You overlook things all the more frequently.

- You overlook significant occasions, for example, arrangements or social commitment.

- You misplace your thought process or the string of discussions, books, or motion pictures.

- You feel progressively overpowered by deciding, arranging steps to achieve an assignment, or getting directions.

The psychological issue is a class of emotional well-being issue that basically influence learning, memory, recognition, and critical thinking, and incorporate amnesia, dementia, and daze. The four significant classifications of psychological issue are wooziness (an adjustment in cognizance that creates over a brief timeframe in which individuals have a decreased attention to their condition); dementia (a dynamic weakening of mind work that is set apart by impedance of memory, perplexity and powerlessness to focus; amnesia (a noteworthy loss of the memory, notwithstanding no loss of other subjective capacities like there is in dementia; and intellectual issue not generally determined (psychological hindrance dared to be because of a general ailment or substance use and doesn't fit into different classifications). The intellectual issue is characterized as any confusion that fundamentally hinders the psychological capacity of a person to the point where ordinary working in the public eye is unimaginable without treatment. Some normal subjective issue incorporates Dementia, Developmental issue, Motor expertise issue, Amnesia, Substance-actuated psychological debilitation.

- You begin to experience difficulty finding your way around well-known conditions.

- You become progressively indiscreet or show progressively misguided thinking.

- Your loved one's notification any of these changes.

In the event that you have MCI, you may likewise be understanding:

•   Depression

•   Irritability and hostility

•   Anxiety

•   Apathy

Causes

Mind shrinkage

There's no single reason for gentle intellectual weakness (MCI), similarly as there's no single result for the turmoil. Side effects of MCI may stay stable for a considerable length of time, progress to Alzheimer's malady or another sort of dementia, or improve after some time. Momentum proof shows that MCI regularly, yet not generally, creates from a lesser level of similar kinds of cerebrum changes found in Alzheimer's sickness or different types of dementia. A portion of these progressions has been recognized in the examination investigations of individuals with MCI.

These progressions include:

•   Abnormal bunches of beta-amyloid protein (plaques) and minuscule protein clusters of tau normal for Alzheimer's sickness (tangles)

•   Lewy bodies, which are minute bunches of another protein related to Parkinson's ailment, dementia with Lewy bodies and a few instances of Alzheimer's illness

•   Small strokes or decreased blood move through mind veins

Mind imaging thinks about the show that the accompanying changes might be related to MCI:

•   Shrinkage of the hippocampus, a cerebrum area significant for memory

•   Enlargement of the cerebrum's liquid occupied spaces (ventricles)

•   Reduced utilization of glucose, the sugar that is the essential wellspring of vitality for cells, in key cerebrum areas

Hazard factors

The most grounded hazard factors for MCI are:

•   Increasing age

•   Having a particular type of a quality known as APOE-e4, additionally connected to Alzheimer's sickness — however, having the quality doesn't ensure that you'll encounter subjective decay

Other ailments and way of life factors have been connected to an expanded danger of intellectual change, including:

•   Diabetes

•   Smoking

•   High circulatory strain

•   Elevated cholesterol

•   Obesity

•   Depression

•   Lack of physical exercise

•   Low instruction level

- Infrequent cooperation in rationally or socially invigorating exercises

Confusions

Individuals with MCI have an essentially expanded hazard — however, not a sureness — of creating dementia. By and large, around 1 to 3 percent of more seasoned grown-ups create dementia consistently. Studies recommend that around 10 to 15 percent of people with MCI proceed to create dementia every year.

CHAPTER FOUR

DEPRESSION

Misery (significant burdensome issue) is a standard and serious ailment that unfavorably impacts how you feel, how you accept, and the manner in which you carry on. Fortunately, it's additionally treatable. Sadness triggers sentiments of misery or a decrease of enthusiasm for exercises once delighted in. It might bring about a wide range of mental and physical issues and can lessen a person's ability to work at work and in your home.

Discouragement indications can differ from moderate to serious and may comprise:

- Feeling tragic or utilizing a desolate state of mind

- Loss of intrigue or joy in exercises once appreciated

- Changes in hunger - weight reduction or

increase helpful for abstaining from excessive food
intake

- Trouble dozing or resting excessively

- Reduction of vitality or expanded weakness

- Boost in purposeless physical activity (e.g.,
hand-wringing or pacing) or eased back developments
and address (activities unmistakable by others)

- Feeling dishonorable or liable

- Difficulty thinking, focusing or deciding

- Thoughts of suicide or passing

Indications need to suffer in any event fourteen days to
get a determination of despondency.

Furthermore, restorative illnesses (e.g., thyroid Issues,
a mind Tumor or nutrient lack) can emulate indications
of discouragement, so it's urgent to preclude general
therapeutic causes. Discouragement influences an
expected 1 of every 15 grown-ups (6.7percent) in Any
schedule year. What's more, one out of six people
(16.6percent) will encounter despondency eventually
in their lifetime. Wretchedness can hit at any minute;

however typically, it first shows up through the late youngsters to mid-20s. Young ladies are to some degree more inclined than men to encounter sadness. A few examinations uncover that 33% of young ladies will encounter a critical burdensome scene in their lifetime.

Melancholy Differs By Sadness or Grief/Bereavement

The death of a friend or family member, loss of a task, or the finish of a Dating are hard encounters for a person to persevere. It's regular for sentiments of depression or sadness to create in response to these situations. Those encountering misfortune every now and again may depict themselves as being"miserable." Be that as it may, being hopeless isn't equivalent to misery. The Grieving procedure is common and one of a kind to each individual and offers some of the exceptionally same attributes of despairing. Both sadness and despairing may include outrageous despondency and withdrawal from ordinary exercises. They're likewise unique in critical manners:

- In despair, difficult sentiments land in waves, frequently intermixed with good recollections of their perishing. Insignificant melancholy, intrigue, or disposition (happiness) are lessened for the majority of fourteen days.

- In despair, confidence is commonly protected. Insignificant misery, sentiments of uselessness, and self-hatred are average.

- For a few people, the death of a friend or family member may cause significant sorrow. Losing employment or turning into a casualty of a physical assault or a huge fiasco may bring about wretchedness for various individuals. At the point when gloom and despairing coincide, the misery is substantially more extreme and endures more than despair without despairing. Regardless of some cover among gloom and despairing, they're particular. Recognizing them can assist people with getting the assistance, backing or treatment they need.

Hazard Factors for Anxiety

Despondency can influence anybody - even Someone Who appears to Live in similarly perfect conditions.

A few variables can assume a job in melancholy:

•	Biochemistry: Differences in specific substances in mind can prompt manifestations of despondency.

•	Genetics: Depression can run in families. By the method, for example, on the off chance that one indistinguishable twin has despairing, another has a 70 percent probability of getting the sickness throughout everyday life.

•	Disposition: Individuals with diminished confidence, who can be promptly overpowered by uneasiness, or who are ordinarily negative appear to be bound to encounter melancholy.

•	Environmental factors: Continuous introduction to brutality, disregard, destitution, or misuse can cause a few people increasingly powerless against wretchedness.

How Is Depression Treated?

Sadness is one of the most treatable of mental diseases. Somewhere in the range of 80% and 90% of people with gloom, at last, react well to treatment. For all intents and purposes, all patients get some help from their side effects.

Before a finding or treatment, a wellbeing expert Should run an intensive demonstrative assessment, for example, a meeting and perhaps a physical appraisal. In some cases, a blood test might be done so as to make sure that the downturn isn't a direct result of an ailment, for example, a thyroid issue. The test is to decide certain indications, family and medicinal history, social elements, and natural elements to land at a conclusion and plan a procedure.

Medication: Brain Chemistry can offer ascent to a person's despairing and may factor in their treatment.

Along these lines, antidepressants might be recommended to help modify the cerebrum science. These drugs aren't sedatives,"uppers" or sedatives. They aren't propensity shaping. Regularly energizer drugs don't have any animating impact on people, not experiencing wretchedness.

Antidepressants may make some advance inside the First week or two of utilization. Absolute advantages probably won't be seen for only a little while. At the point when a patient feels close to nothing in the event that any improvement following half a month, at that point, her or his therapist can change the portion of this medication or substitute or include another upper. In specific cases, other psychotropic drugs may be valuable. It's imperative to inform your doctor as to whether a medication doesn't work or on the off chance that you experience undesirable reactions.

Therapists, by and large, prescribe that patients keep on ingesting medications for two or three months following indications have improved. Longer-term care treatment might be demonstrated to bring down the likelihood of future scenes for explicit individuals at raised hazard.

Psychotherapy: Psychotherapy, or"talk treatment," can be utilized solely for the treatment of moderate sorrow; for moderate to serious despondency, psychotherapy is habitually used in joined with upper medications. Subjective social treatment (CBT) has been demonstrated to be effective in relieving despondency. CBT is a sort of treatment concentrated on current and critical thinking. CBT encourages a person to perceive twisted reasoning and change thinking and practices. Psychotherapy may include only the individual, yet it might incorporate others. By the method, for example, couples or family treatment may help address issues inside these personal connections. Gathering treatment includes people with comparable afflictions. In view of the seriousness of the downturn, treatment can Simply take a long time or more. Customarily, noteworthy advancement can be come to in 10 to 15 sessions. Electroconvulsive Therapy (ECT) is a restorative treatment most normally utilized for people with intense Major wretchedness or bipolar issue who haven't reacted to different treatments. It involves a short electric incitement of the mind while the patient is under anesthesia. An individual commonly gets ECT 2 to multiple times every week for a sum of six to 12 medicines. ECT was utilized as the 1940s, and loads of long periods of study have added to critical enhancements. It's ordinarily dealt with by a gathering of prepared parental figures, for example, an analyst, an anesthesiologist, and a medical caretaker or doctor partner.

Self-improvement and Dealing

There are various things people can do to help decrease The markers of despondency. For many individuals, normal exercise helps produce positive inclination and upgrade state of mind. Getting enough phenomenal rest on a typical premise, eating a healthy eating regimen, and keeping away from liquor (a depressant) may likewise lessen the side effects of despondency. Gloom is a genuine sickness, and help can be gotten. With Good recognizable proof and treatment, the incredible greater part of people with gloom will vanquish it. In case you're having indications of sadness, stage one comprehends your family specialist or analyst. Discussion about your interests and ask for an extensive assessment. This is a starting to tending to psychological wellness needs. There has been an incredible increment in mental issues and variations from the norm throughout the most recent years. The predominance of medication use, both therapeutic and 'recreational,' has been a solid contributory factor alongside expanded liquor utilization, mechanical and concoction contamination, and numerous different components. The sad predominance of upsetting everyday news demonstrating a general multiplication of savagery in news reports adds to an unwholesome image of the world in which we live. This can have a discouraging effect upon our brains or can center the need to think about the reasons for such an increment in psychological sickness in the network and to look for a cure. Early instruction is significant when showing limitations in the utilization of medications, both medicinal and recreational, alongside the damaging impact of liquor. Together with guidance about the indispensable need to sustain our psyches with healthy considerations would no uncertainty help youthful ones later on. In any case, for the 20% of the populace previously enduring mental issue, this gives little encouragement. Those of us who might be on edge that our perspective isn't typical can counsel a clinician who will prompt us or suggest a specialist if that is demonstrated. Anyway, in first viewing self as a conclusion, it might be useful, yet not really along these lines, to know about a portion of the anomalies that might be foreseen as basic in our very own sort of character. The extraordinary attributes of each kind are outstanding, for example, the doubt and ridiculous question of a jumpy; the lacking limit with regards to the love of a schizoid; the over-emotional responses and articulations of a theatrical; or the narcissistic sorts of individuals who are conceited in the outrageous. These are just those couple of kinds of a character known and treated in psychiatry. The majority of us can, in specific conditions, show brief examples of any or all unpredictable social articulations, so we should take care not to overstate any inclination we may have. We should hold good judgment in making a decision about our own perspective and know whether our manifestations start to show that the time has come to look for help from an expert. As guardians or carers, we likewise should attempt to decide, in the interest of those in our consideration, regardless of whether we should look for proficient assistance for their sake. This need is evident in the psychopathic character when it can create forceful conduct from the get-go in existence with a propensity to mishandle other youngsters or creatures or to show defiant or remorseless conduct. These youngsters, if not helped, will in grown-up life, in general, become uncivilized and outrage by viciousness or some likeness thereof. Be that as it may, in another way, we can say, following individual self-assessment, that in general, we are agreeable inside ourselves; that we see that our constructive character and character characteristics exceed the antagonistic ones and that we can decide to improve with use of self-restraint, at that point, there appears to be little to stress over however to proceed with self-culture of our constructive and sound character.

Sydney is one of the greatest and most populated urban areas of Australia. The city is home to probably the best youngster analysts on the planet. In the present upsetting life, numerous youngsters in Sydney are confronting various mental issues. A kid faces numerous sorts of issues, of which some they can deal with alone while others need extraordinary consideration. The majority of the occasions, such issues can be treated through analyst's recommendations and customary check-ups, yet in some cases, a kid may require neurofeedback. Neurofeedback Sydney is really a learning procedure to improve the capacity of the mind. The procedure is compelling for ADHD treatment and different other learning issues. Youngsters who are experiencing this issue are delayed in learning and have a low degree of fixation. Furthermore, they likewise give different indications of resting issues. The neurofeedback really creates brainwaves that are exceptionally compelling in adjusting the development of the kid's mind. The treatment has ended up being helpful for kids who are experiencing ADHD issues. Neurofeedback is compelling and doesn't have any hurtful impact on the youngster's mind. Your kid won't become a junkie to the procedure as there are no addictive medications included. The entire procedure takes around a half year to finish, yet positive outcomes are ensured. The procedure will improve its fixation level and make them less rash. For getting the best outcomes, you should pursue the total procedure carefully. Then again, an enormous number of individuals all over Sydney are experiencing nervousness issues. This issue has numerous passionate, social, and physical side effects. An individual experiencing the turmoil can feel uneasy and dreadful about his own life. He may likewise encounter some chest torment and absence of fixation. Furthermore, he may act unusually by abstaining from visiting certain spots with no explanation. Different treatments like presentation treatment, deliberate desensitization and subjective conduct treatment are demonstrated to be advantageous against this issue. A sleeping disorder is really a resting issue in which an individual can't rest in any event, when he needs to. The greatest reason for this issue is pressure and strain. Aside from this, dread and uneasiness are different reasons for this issue. A sleeping disorder offers to ascend to numerous other medical issues like hypertension, low focus levels and diabetes. An ideal approach to keep a sleeping disorder under control is the psychological conduct treatment regularly rehearsed by Child Psychologist Sydney. This treatment is an ideal approach to totally kill this issue. There are different meds also, yet these may have some symptoms. We give absolute consultancy and treatment to different mental issues; subsequently, in the event that you or your kid is experiencing any such issue, at that point call today.

Treatment Options - Drugs vs. Therapy

Consistently in the UK, a great many individuals are determined to have regular mental issues. The consciousness of basic mental issues is expanding because of presentation through various types of media. This remembers storylines for premium dramas just as government battles. Progressively the marks of disgrace joined to these disarranges are vanishing and individuals are increasingly open in their endeavors to look for help for them. Treatment for normal mental issue arrives in a wide range of structures. A few people pick altogether for a medications disease though others decide on the treatment course, and at times is it seen as reasonable to join the two. The patient can settle on drugs if a specialist thinks t is pertinent, though treatment can be gone without a specialist authorization. By and large, the patient will want to get referral trough a specialist with the goal that they can acquire treatment at a limited rate or for nothing out of pocket.

The following is a breakdown of the upsides and downsides of the distinctive treatment alternatives accessible for the normal mental issue:

Medications

The medication alternatives are accessible to the patient contrast contingent upon the mental issue that is available, or is suspected to be available. By and large the patient will be begun a little portion before bit by bit expanding to what is viewed as a dose that is best in that specific case. This is to condition the body to the medication and to limit any potential reactions.

Aces

• Medicine is demonstrated to normally have the ideal outcome when utilized in the right measurements and at significant occasions, despite the fact that this isn't ensured.

• The medication can go about as a sofa-bed to the patient. It can have a misleading impact where the patient feels significantly better only for having taken it.

• This technique for treatment can without much of a stretch be managed and controlled; on the off chance that it isn't working, at that point, the patient can simply quit taking the medication.

• Doctors currently have immense experience in utilizing these medications as they are so normal.

Cons

• Drugs can frequently have symptoms, in spite of the fact that not all individuals experience these. These symptoms can be at their generally noticeable toward the beginning of the course of medication when the body isn't utilized to the substance and is adjusting to its essence in the framework.

• The patient can get subject to the medication, and the ide,a of halting the course of medication can cause a mental issue in itself.

Treatment

Professionals:

• Therapy doesn't have any reactions and can, without much of a stretch, be halted.

• It is beneficial to converse with individuals about your issues who are understanding and thoughtful.

• A rightful method for building certainty.

• Therapists are experts in the field and have a huge involvement in managing mental issues.

Cons

• It can be scary to venture out.

• It can be disappointing in the event that you don't feel you taxi legitimize your issue to the advisor

• Therapy can't settle natural issues, for example, a compound awkwardness of the cerebrum, implying that it isn't constantly significant.

• It can require some investment to get results

We regularly hear the expression "Misery" as it's much

of the time used to portray a mind-set or feeling. The dismal pity of despondency barely needs portrayal, so basic is its part in the human condition. In specialized terms, it is portrayed as an indication of a disorder or mental issue and just the length isolates the disposition from the manifestation. At the point when this sentiment of discouragement is available reliably for significant stretches of time, it is viewe,d as a side effect of a burdensome issue. There is a long convention of arranging melancholy into types, and there are various analytic plans at present being used. The DSM (Diagnostic and Statistical Manual) has, for some time, been the transcendent analytic structure utilized by analysts and therapists in North America now for a very long while.

Significant Depression

This is the thing that individuals have as a main priority when alluding to "clinical wretchedness." When the side effects of sadness are available and noteworthy for the vast majority of the day, at any rate, and for at least 2 weeks, they may have a Major Depression. This class of wretchedness is additionally separated into Major Depressive Disorder Single Episode and Recurrent subtypes.

Dysthymia

This is a by and large milder, yet all the more suffering kind of wretchedness. While Sufferers may not display their side effects each day, yet rather on most days for a time of at any rate two years.

Bipolar Disorder

In the past known as Manic Depression, in Bipolar issue, people either substitute burdensome lows with hyper or hypomanic up-swings or experience a purported "blended mindset states" where they display highlights of sorrow and insanity simultaneously.

Change Disorder with Depressed Mood

Some time ago perceived as "receptive sorrow," this is

a burdensome reaction to an actual existence stress that is more extreme than anticipated for the sort of stress experienced.

Occasional Affective Disorder

Frequently talked about in the media as though it is an exceptional issue, this is a variety of either sorrow or bipolar issue where the scenes match with regular changes.

Insane Depression

This is a variety of Major Depression where, with expanded seriousness, insane side effects (e.g., pipedreams, daydreams) are displayed.

Post-birth anxiety

Another variety of Major Depression that is accelerated by labor in ladies. While not typically applied to men, a baby blues response among new fathers may be better represented as a change issue, or comprehended as far as "division tension." While some are less influenced by sadness, others may endure enormously. We trust this article gave some understanding about a different issue and if do experience the ill effects of any of these don't spare a moment to a certified proficient for help.

CHAPTER FIVE

PANIC DISORDER

An individual encountering a fit of anxiety feels an evident influx of dread for no specific explanation by any means. The individual heart starts to pulsate quickly, his chest hurt, and it becomes progressively increasingly hard to inhale, at which time the individual accepts he is having respiratory failure and will bite the dust on the off chance that he doesn't get appropriate intercession. One patient characterized his side effects along these lines: I am so apprehensive; each time I begin to go out I get that dreadful inclination in the pit of my stomach, and I am scared that another fit of anxiety is coming or that some other obscure awful thing will transpire or somebody in my family." The fit of anxiety by and large lasts close to a couple of moments; however, it very well may be the most troubling condition that a person can understand. People who experienced one assault will have others. The individuals who experience rehashed assaults or feel elevated nervousness about having another assault are considered to have created an alarm issue.

Frenzy issue is a genuine medical issue in the United States. Ongoing examinations presumed that around 3,000,000 individuals would encounter alarm assaults sooner or later during their lives. The side effect is strikingly not quite the same as different kinds of nervousness. Fits of anxiety are exceptionally abrupt and regularly unforeseen, apparently unwarranted, and are frequently crippling. The fit of anxiety can happen whenever, in any event, during rest. An assault regularly tops inside ten minutes, yet a few side effects may last any longer.

What causes alarm assaults: And how would you treat alarm issue?

One way to deal with understanding the reason for alarm issue is that the body's typical caution framework the psychological and physical systems that enables an individual to respond to a risk, will, in general, be activated superfluously, when there is no genuine threat in the prompt condition. Most medicinal examinations can't clarify precisely why this occurs. Be that as it may, a few mental investigations have appeared, the underlying driver of frenzy issue may starts on the enthusiastic level or the physical side, or it could be both. The sentiment of uplifted tension consistently starts with a trigger that starts the battle or flight reaction from the limbic framework. For instance, the main trace of obvious risk your mind science, blood hormones, and cell digestion all goes without hesitation. At the point when you have an interminable tension issue after some time, your uneasiness side effects might be activated by less and less genuine occasions in light of the fact that the limbic framework has been sharpened to respond in an exceptionally panicky way. For instance, if as a kid you were continually hollered at; as a grown-up, you may feel on edge at whatever point there is potential for encounter with a position figure; and you may go to extraordinary measures to maintain a strategic distance from such showdown, even in a circumstance as favorable as declining a basic solicitation by a relative or anybody of power figure. Now your cognizant personality has forgotten about the association between your present inclination and your past enthusiastic experience. You currently have no clue why you are feeling panicky about something of so minimal huge.

Past passionate experience

Early passionate encounters are the origination for the advancement of frenzy issue. The experience may have been early youth injury, for example, the passing of a parent, separate, kid misuse, steady analysis, surrender, hardship, or an exceptionally enthusiastic family social condition; profoundly on edge guardians, including alcoholic and medication dependent guardians. Youth is a period of little power and control. At the point when terrible things happen to kids, their methods for dealing with stress are not completely created; they can't process what had occurred in a wellbeing way and proceed onward. Undeniably, these unfavorable youth encounters are caught profound inside. As a grown-ups, those concealed issues regularly surface as nervousness side effects. It might be hard to associate what is setting off your frenzy state to your past encounters, yet there, s constantly a connection.

Past experience has instructed me that you shouldn't endeavor to treat alarm issue except if you are happy to address it from numerous sides; this methodology can be tedious and passionate escalated work, which customary professionals, over and over again, will, in general, maintain a strategic distance from. Rather, antidepressants are given out like treat to freeze patients to quiet their physical side effects. Be that as it may, it doesn't make a difference what kind of frenzy side affects you are encountering you should address the passionate segment if indication decrease is to be accomplished.

Method of medicines

There is a wide assortment of medicines accessible for alarm issue, including a few compelling psychopharmacology intercessions, and explicit types of psychotherapy. Psychotherapy for alarm issue is similarly significant as medication intercession. A few examinations the blend of prescription and psychotherapy treatment for alarm issue is more viable than either intercession alone.

Subjective Behavioral Therapy (CBT) is broadly acknowledged as the predominant type of psychotherapy. CBT is intended to help those with alarm issues distinguish and decline the nonsensical contemplations and practices that strengthen alarm side effects. Psychodynamic psychotherapy is another type of intercession that is only from time to time referenced as a fitting treatment for alarm issues. Truth be told, numerous specialists emphatically dismiss utilizing psychodynamic procedures as an intercession to decrease the manifestations related with an alarm issues. What sets psycho dynamic specialists apart from the rest is their capacity to remember one unquestionable actuality: Panic states may, symptomatically, have all the earmarks of being indistinguishable climate they are produced from a masochist condition or from a hyper burdensome state.

Clinical research showed that hypochondriac sort of frenzy states ought to be dealt with exclusively with psychotherapy, and hyper burdensome states are to be treated with one of the numerous powerful enemies of burdensome medications. Legitimate differential determination is the super-roadway to indication a decrease for every mental issue, including an alarm issue.

Treating alarm issue with psychodynamic procedures in spite of the fact that reviews have demonstrated the viability of subjective social and psychopharmacological medicines, numerous patients neglect to react emphatically to these mediations or have had tirelessness or repeat of side effects. Given the significant expenses and return of frenzy disorder, there is a need to investigate treatment alternatives. Psychoanalytic methods are generally used to treat alarm issues yet have once in a while been presented to the meticulousness of logical research systems. Such an examination would feature and portray the psychoanalytic ideas engaged with understanding frenzy issue. While simultaneously proposes a more "customer inviting" psychodynamic psychotherapy for alarm issue called alarm centered psychodynamic psychotherapy. The potential advantage of this type of treatment depends on the conviction that frenzy patients have mental helplessness to freeze issues related to character aggravations, relationship issues, challenges enduring and characterizing inward passionate encounters, and oblivious clashes about partition, outrage and sexuality. Psychodynamic psychotherapy concentrates more, however not only, on these weaknesses than different treatments, including psychopharmacology, possibly diminishing helplessness to side effects repeat.

Oblivious feelings

As per psychoanalytic hypothesis, alarm indications are put together in any event to some degree with respect to oblivious dreams and influences; actually, both clinical and explore perception recommends that frenzy patients have extraordinary challenges with outrage emotions and dreams, for example, want for vengeance. These desires regularly speak to a danger to significant loved ones, particularly those we have a nearby connection to, subsequently setting off a fit of anxiety. Patients are regularly ignorant of the intensity of these effects and the vindictive dreams that go with them. Getting mindful, by carry them to awareness of these negative parts of mental life and render them less undermining, are significant segments of psychodynamic psychotherapy.

How Anxiety Disorders Can Be Treated

A wide assortment of clutters identified with

nervousness, pressure, stress and dread are commonly named uneasiness issues. The particular sorts incorporate frenzy issue and fears or silly apprehensions. The power of the manifestations experienced by individuals experiencing may change one individual to another. Stress, awful accidents, and dread are the absolute most normal factors that can trigger the advancement of the clutters. An individual encountering may experience the ill effects of explicit responses of the body including unreasonable perspiring, heart palpitation, migraines, and extraordinary weariness. The more extreme the uneasiness assault turns into, the more fragile the individual would be. People inclined to tension issue ought to consistently go with others, just in the event that an uneasiness assault happens whenever at that point nervousness issue treatment can be pursued.

Sadness, from gentle to major, and other mental issue have likewise been connected to nervousness issues. Nervousness issue is regularly brought about by covering factors, in this way, outlining the turmoil from other mental issues would be troublesome. Articles and others are a portion of the natural factors that fill in as triggers for the scatters. Indeed, even boosts that are not typically destructive, for example, butterflies can cause uneasiness and outrageous dread for people encountering tension issues. Having a confusion would be especially upsetting in light of the fact that each experience would lead with the activating improvement that would prompt an assault. On the off chance that you speculate that somebody you know is experiencing it, you can watch the shared characteristics among all their assaults for you to distinguish what explicit improvements triggers the confusion. The degree of the confusion can be dictated by counseling a specialist or a clinician. Counseling a specialist is viewed as the initial phase in endeavoring to treat or fix the turmoil. The individual enduring experiences a mental treatment with the goal that the person would have the option to conquer their uneasiness or dread each time the person in question experiences the activating upgrade. Treating a tension issues is frequently adopted through two distinct strategies: intellectual or social. The pervasive contemplations of a person during the tension assault fill in as the notable purpose of intellectual methodologies in treating the scatters. Through this striking point, the specialist can recognize the chain of feeling that fills in as the prelude to the ascent or improvement of nervousness issue. The other methodology, the social procedures, concentrates more on the conduct responses of the person to the particular occasions or circumstances activated by the assault. On the off chance that these two methodologies would be joined, the odds that the confusion would be dealt with are higher. Besides treatment, an analyst or therapist may likewise prescribe the admission of specific meds. In any case, a significant disadvantage in accepting drugs as treatment for the scatters and another mental issues is the certainty of symptoms. A withdrawal disorder may likewise grow once the admission has been halted. Besides, taking prescriptions may likewise lead the person to be subject to the medication, conceivably prompting substance misuse. Frenzy issue is a mental condition that is portrayed by monotonous fits of anxiety. The principal manifestation of frenzy issue is fit of anxiety which is an arbitrary rush of extraordinary and overpowering apprehension and nervousness that keep going for a couple of moments to 60 minutes.

Understanding Panic Disorder

In countless cases, alarm scenes strike all of a sudden, without notice. A fit of anxiety is arbitrary and consequently, it happens anyplace whenever, without incitement. It could even happen when a patient is at rest. The fit of anxiety, in various cases, is a one-time occasion despite the fact that in most the occurrences, it is a dull cycle. Individuals who have encountered a fit of anxiety before are bound to encounter them once more. For the most part, alarm scenes occur in explicit circumstances where they have a first show or under conditions that make it liable to happen, for example, swarmed spots and circumstances where departure might be troublesome or unthinkable. Individuals who are encountering alarm assaults, notwithstanding having the condition, are generally physically sound yet not really alive and well. In any case, the alarm issue regularly goes with other mental issues or concerns, for example, fears, despondency and nervousness issues.

Side effects

An individual encountering a frenzy scene experience issues breathing, feel bleary-eyed, has sporadic heartbeat, is wiped out to the stomach and may have manifestations like those accomplished by individuals having a coronary failure. Most patients depict the indications as having a mind-boggling feeling of going insane or a looming fate. No big surprise, it is frequently portrayed as among the most seriously startling experience an individual could live through. An all-out fit of anxiety and confusion incorporates a mix of the accompanying side effects:

Physical: Shortness of breath or hypoventilation, sentiment of being gagged, chest torment or distress, resentful stomach, shaking or trembling, hot or cold flushes, and shivering sensations all through the body.

Mental: Sense of going insane, of kicking the bucket or of being 'scattered,' feeling of losing control, and unreasonable inclination all through the body.

You might be managing the condition on the off chance that you:
I have had a fit of anxiety at any rate once.
Stress too much over an approaching scene of fit of anxiety.
Alter your conduct as a consequence of dread or nervousness over encountering a frenzy scene.

Causes

The accurate reasons for alarm issues are not yet distinguished. Be that as it may, specialists concur that it runs in the family, it is straightforwardly connected to significant conditions throughout one's life and is profoundly established in awful encounters. It might likewise root from explicit ailments, for example, hyperthyroidism, hypoglycemia, utilization of substances, withdrawal from drugs and mitral valve prolapse.

Medicines for Panic Disorder

There are treatment and treatment alternatives for the alternatives. Among the treatment that produce the best outcomes are:

Intellectual conduct treatment or CBT - This is conceivably the best treatment for alarm issues and is frequently utilized for the treatment of fear, tension issue and different types of fear. This treatment technique centers around fixing the examples of conduct and feeling that incite and support a fit of anxiety. It gives patients to see their feelings of trepidation and nerves access an increasingly reasonable light.

Introduction treatment - This is a method that attempts to reproduce the real conditions that trigger an assault in a controlled situation. The goal of this treatment is to assist patients with shaping more advantageous methods for dealing with the stress they could utilize when a genuine assault occurs outside of a controlled situation.

Different alternatives for treating alarm issues incorporate the utilization of drugs and self-improvement procedures.

CHAPTER SIX

STRESS

The American Psychological Association (APA) characterizes Stress as"a feeling portrayed by sentiments of uneasiness, focused on thoughts and real changes like an improved pulse." Understanding the qualification between ordinary sentiments of stress and A nervousness issue requiring restorative consideration can assist somebody with recognizing and care for the issue. In this guide, we take a gander at the holes among pressure And stress issues, the few sorts of pressure, and the accessible treatment decisions.

When does pressure need treatment?

While stress can lead to trouble, It's not really an ailment.

Stress

When a Person faces potentially destructive or focusing on Triggers, sentiments of stress aren't simply ordinary yet vital for endurance. Since the principal long periods of mankind, the procedure of Predators and approaching risk sets off alerts inside the human body and empowers hesitant activity. These alarms become clear in the sort of an expanded heartbeat, perspiring, and expanded affectability to condition. The risk causes a surge of adrenalin, a hormone, and Chemical envoy in the cerebrum, which in this way actuates these anxious responses in a method known as the"fight-or-flight' reaction. This gets ready people to go up against or avoid any potential threats to security. For a Lot of People, running from greater creatures and approaching Threat is a less squeezing worry than it may have been for old individuals. Tensions at present rotate around work, cash, family life, wellbeing, and other basic issues that require a person's concentration without continually requiring the 'fight-or-flight' reaction. The anxious inclination preceding a noteworthy life occasion or through a difficult situation is a characteristic reproduction of their first' fight-or-flight' reaction. It might, in any case, be pivotal to endurance - the dread of being struck by a vehicle when going across the street, as an example, infers that an individual will naturally look the two different ways to counteract risk.

Stress issue

The length or seriousness of an on edge environment can Occasionally be out of extent to the underlying reason or stressor. Physical signs, for example, raised circulatory strain and queasiness, and may likewise develop. These criticism continue past apprehension to a pressure issue. The APA portrays an Individual with nervousness ailment as "having repeating nosy considerations or stresses." Once dread reaches the purpose of an illness, it might meddle with every day working.

Indications

Despite the fact that various examinations establish tension Disorders, the manifestations of summed up uneasiness issue (GAD) will much of the time incorporate these:

- Restlessness, and a feeling of being "on-edge."
- Uncontrollable sentiments of stress
- Increased touchiness
- Concentration issues
- Sleep issues, similar to challenges in falling or staying snoozing

While these side effects May Be ordinary to encounter everyday Life, people with GAD will experience them to determined or extraordinary sums. Stray may present excessively unclear, waiting for stress or even an increasingly intense tension that intrudes on day by day living.

Types

Frenzy issue is a Sort of nervousness issue.

The Diagnostic and Statistical Manual of Mental Health Diseases: Fifth Edition (DSM-V) characterizes anxiety issues into a few principle structures. In past renditions of DSM, stress issue included over the top habitual issue (OCD) and post-awful nervousness issue (PTSD), notwithstanding serious pressure ailment. Then again, the guide now no more classes these mental medical problems under pressure.

Stress issues today incorporate the after findings.

Summed up nervousness issue: This truly is a constant disease including exorbitant, long haul Stress, and tensions about vague life occasions, things, and circumstances. Stray is the most widely recognized tension issue, and people with the infection aren't constantly ready to detect the purpose behind the pressure. Uneasiness issue: Sudden or unforeseen assaults of extraordinary fear and nervousness depict alarm issues. These assaults can cause vibration, queasiness, disarray, sickness, and breathing issues.

Fits of anxiety tend to occur and heighten rapidly, cresting the following 10 minutes. In any case, a fit of anxiety could keep going for a considerable length of time. Frenzy issue for the most part occur subsequent to startling encounters Or delayed pressure, however, may likewise occur with no reason. Somebody experiencing a fit of anxiety can misjudge it as a hazardous sickness and might roll out radical improvements in conduct to avert future assaults.

<u>Explicit fear:</u> This can be a nonsensical dread and shirking of a particular thing or circumstance. Fears aren't caring for other nervousness issues, as they identify with a specific reason. Somebody with fear may concede a frenzy as Illogical or extraordinary yet remain incapable of controlling emotions anxiety around the reason. Triggers for a fear extend in the situations and critters to ordinary things.

<u>Agoraphobia:</u> This Is a frenzy and shirking of regions, occasions, or circumstances where it could be difficult to escape or at which help wouldn't be accessible if an individual gets caught. We frequently misjudge this

sickness for fear of accessible spaces and the outside, yet it isn't excessively clear. Somebody who has agoraphobia can have a dread of venturing out from home or with lifts and open transportation.

<u>Specific mutism:</u> This is a kind of stress that a few youngsters experience, where they're not able to talk in specific zones or settings, for example, school, in spite of the way that they may have uncommon verbal, relational abilities around well-known people. It could be an outrageous type of social tension.

<u>Social tension issue, or social uneasiness:</u> This truly is a dread of unfriendly judgment from others in cultural Scenarios or of open mortification. Social uneasiness issue contains an assortment of emotions, similar to organize trepidation, a dread of closeness, and anxiety around dismissal and mortification. This sickness can make individuals avoid open Circumstances And human touch to the phase that standard living is left amazingly hard. Division nervousness issue: High degrees of worry after partition by an Individual or spot that Provides sentiments of wellbeing or security

describe detachment tension issue. Psychotherapy may every so often lead to freezing indications.

Reasons

The foundation of uneasiness issue is intricate. Many may Occur at the same time, some could prompt others, and a couple may not bring about an uneasiness issue except if another exists.

Potential triggers include:

Ecological issues, similar to issues at work, association Issues, or family unit issues Hereditary qualities, as people who have relatives having an uneasiness issue are bound to experience themselves

Wellbeing factors, similar to the Signs of confusion, the results of a medication, or the uneasiness of serious activity or extended recuperation

Cerebrum science, as clinicians determine a few pressure issue as misalignments of hormones and electrical flag in the mind

Withdrawal from an illicit substance, the implications

of that may hamper the effect of extra potential causes

Treatment

Medications will incorporate a mix of psychotherapy, Behavioral treatment, and medications. Liquor compulsion, despairing , or elective Conditions can once in a while have such an amazing impact on mental prosperity, which treating a tension issue needs to hold up till any inborn diseases are brought under administration.

Self-treatment

Yoga can lessen the impacts of a pressure issue.

Some of the time, Someone can fix a pressure issue at Home without clinical oversight. All things considered, this probably won't be effective for intense or long haul pressure issues. There Are Lots of activities and exercises to enable a man To manage milder, increasingly thought, or shorter-term uneasiness issue, for example:

1.   Pressure administration: figuring out how to oversee pressure will help confine potential causes. Arrange any inevitable cutoff times and weights, gather records to acquire overwhelming occupations significantly more reasonable, and commit to taking a break from study or work.

2.   Comfort strategies: Simple activities can help kill the mental and physiological indications of stress. These techniques incorporate reflection, profound breathing activities, long washrooms, resting in obscurity, and yoga.

3.   Exercises to supplant negative considerations with positive ones: Create a rundown of those negative thoughts that might be biking as a result of pressure, and compose another rundown adjacent to it containing hopeful, trustworthy plans to substitute them. Building up a mental picture of effectively standing up to and beating a specific dread may likewise give focal points if stress indications identify with a specific reason, as in fear.

4.   Support people group: Speak with conspicuous

people that are strong, similar to a family member or companion. Care group administrations may likewise be accessible at the neighborhood on the web.

5.   Exercise: Physical effort may improve mental self-portrait and release synthetic compounds in the cerebrum that trigger positive feelings. It has been known for quite a while that negative feelings are attached to explicit illnesses - for example, fears lead to cardiovascular illnesses, outrage harms the liver, lack of concern influences the stomach. They all share something for all intents and purpose - stress. Be that as it may, by what method would it be a good idea for us to manage the pressure?

What is pressure? For what reason does it occur? Is it in every case awful?

Stress is an unavoidable piece of regular day to day existence. Minor burdens are innocuous (and even supportive now and again); in any case, negative, dependable pressure can be weakening to one's wellbeing. The creator of the hypothesis of stress, surely understood Canadian researcher Hans Selye, has decided worry as a lot of average hereditarily modified vague responses of a life form went for its endurance by methods for its "battle or flight" reaction. Minor impacts of negative components don't as a rule cause pressure. It happens when the pressure factors (stressors) outperform our regular capacity to deal with them. The stressors cause the body to change its method for working by activating its assets to adapt to risk (raise blood siphoning and widen aviation routes to build oxygen admission, increment blood thickening, and so on.) or adjusting to it. This is the fundamental motivation behind pressure reaction.

A run of the mill pressure reaction has 3 stages:

1.   Alertness - to prepare every defensive mean of the body.

2.   Stabilization - adjusted utilization of the body's versatile capacities.

3.   Exhaustion - last stage coming after the delayed impacts of stressors has spent every single

versatile save of the body.

Some pressure is a characteristic piece of life, which as Selye would see it makes a "sample of life". Stress invigorates us in complex procedures at work, in inventive undertakings, and in rivalry. Be that as it may, when the solid impact of stressors become over the top and consistent, they channel our defensive methods and can prompt ailment, or even reason hypochondriac or psychosomatic issue. Various individuals respond to stressors in an unexpected way. Some respond proactively, battling the peril. Others respond inactively and surrender rapidly. For the most part, these sorts of responses cause explicit kinds of disarranges. In view of various clinical perceptions, specialists have found that most stressors regularly cause hypertension, ulcer, cardiovascular failure, stroke, heart arrhythmias, and so forth. The outrage that isn't communicated could cause rheumatoid joint inflammation, skin issues, headache, acid reflux, and so on. For what reason does pressure cause a substantial issues? At the point when we are feeling solid negative feelings, noteworthy physical changes occur in the body causing unnecessary vitality creation. Additionally, a drawn-out adverse mental frame of mind/character regularly advances quicker fatigue of the body's defensive methods.

Association among stress and infection.

Clinicians and therapists have found a solid association between certain character qualities toward one side and substantial issue on the other. Model: people are attempting to fit in a specific position/work that doesn't accommodate their character or abilities have a higher opportunity to create cardiovascular maladies. The ceaseless coronary malady is increasingly regular for proactive objective situated, goal-oriented and less tolerant people. People experiencing stomach ulcers are regularly extremely on edge and bad-tempered. They are exceptionally scrupulous, yet, for the most part, have low confidence, are a defenseless, bashful, delicate and despondent person. These people consistently attempt to accomplish more than they are prepared to do. They will, in general, conquer challenges having an exceptionally significant level of tension. The degree of stress-related obsessive changes in the body is normally connected with an individual evaluation of the circumstance, which thusly relies upon sentiments of moral obligation. The indications of passionate pressure showing up in unpleasant circumstances will in general, heighten when there is an absence of physical movement.

Stress Disorders.

There is no unequivocal rundown of stress-related issues. A similar sort of infection could have a pressure starting point or could be brought about by something different. A wide range of elements might be joined with the worry in an individual's life that impact bodywork. The mix of negative elements is especially hazardous in light of the fact that it makes more opportunities to build up specific sicknesses. Among the many pressure-related issues the principle ones are depressions - mental irregularity brought about by delayed psycho-enthusiastic experience, mental and physical strain, absence of rest or rest, durable inward battling, repressed sentiments of melancholy, outrage or enduring. Some substantial ailments may cause mental issues too. Mental issues may show up due to having an absence of choices to determine a major issue. It could happen when an individual attempts to determine an issue, however, can't do it. This prompts expanded affectability or crabbiness to the issue making an individual increasingly passionate. This at that point, makes the individual experience different agonies in light of the impact of stressors.

Stress responses are altogether different.

An acceptable degree of passionate addiction causes an individual to perform better. Anyway, delayed enthusiastic strain, in the end, prompts a drop in execution. The more mind-boggling the action is, the speedier the individual gets bothered, causing sentiments of weakness, lack of care, loss of focus, interruption and memory challenges. A few people may respond to worry in an exceptionally dynamic way while others would surrender rapidly. A proactive reaction may prompt on the spot judgment calls that emphasis on just the principal parts of the issue. This hyperactive-habitual response prompts a noteworthy increment in committing errors while the movement stays solid or even expanded. Rather than this, a restrained response prompts more slow reasoning, and increments progress ahead in the learning procedure. The enthusiastic atmosphere at work and home assumes a significant job in keeping up with mental and physical wellbeing. Everyone's state of mind depends a great deal on the temperament of the individuals who encompass him/her, and it appears in their words, emulates and conduct. When speaking with others, one will in general, take on their idealism or sorrow. Along these lines, shared feelings become run of the mill indications of good climate in the gathering of collaborators or relatives. No one is insusceptible from mishaps, key misfortunes or insoluble issues. Be that as it may, it isn't great to concentrate on negative feelings excessively long or let gloom overpower you. For your wellbeing, it is vastly improved to concentrate on attempting to locate a positive arrangement.

Approaches to alleviating pressure.

Isometric activities. This technique depends on putting a strain on specific muscles and afterward loosening up them in a rehashed, cadenced way. A model may be making a clench hand and afterward loosening up it or put your hands behind your head and press it forward stressing neck muscles to drive back, at that point press your feet to the ground and unwind. These basic activities can be utilized in any circumstance to accomplish unwinding. Autogenic preparing. This is a notable technique for unwinding. A profound unwinding that individuals, for the most part feel after spellbinding can be accomplished by methods for self-interesting procedures. You can sit discreetly and give yourself straightforward directions like: I'm feeling quiet, I'm feeling substantial. My arms and legs are feeling warm and overwhelming. To get great at this, you should rehearse it a couple of times. The impact of this system could become more grounded if profound breathing is utilized during the activity. Contemplation. All known contemplation methods are focused on concentrating your considerations and consideration on a solitary thing. It could be music, a mantra or your own relaxing. Every single other idea becomes stopped, and different interruptions are totally disregarded. Such focus encourages you to accomplish a profound unwinding. Profound taking in the mix with a particular sitting stance and shut eyes accomplish a full rest. Biofeedback preparing. For as far back as scarcely any decades, biofeedback has gotten well known among pressure the executive's experts. The idea of biofeedback preparing depends on estimating certain physical parameters that can be legitimately or in a roundabout way controlled. The subject/individual can see the real levels while being given explicit intriguing or controlling directions that influence the parameter being estimated. A model is - skin temperature is by and large constantly estimated while interesting considerations are being actuated intended to loosen up muscles. Muscle unwinding makes fringe veins enlarge and increment bloodstream in appendages, which thus causes skin temperature to rise. The temperature level is being shown to the subject alongside the continuation of giving interesting considerations. Accordingly, the subject sets up a criticism prompting further unwinding. For as far back as decade, an extraordinary biofeedback strategy has increased a lot of consideration in the pressure the executive's field. It depends on utilizing profound cadenced breathing emphatically influencing the heart musicality by making it sway reasonably with breathing pace. This strategy includes a significant physiological system of baroreflex that is answerable for the body's adjustment to different components (physical effort, psycho-passionate burdens) and for accomplishing the body's inward homeostasis. This method is a unique exercise to this instrument, via preparing and conditioning it along these lines to physical exercise for muscles and cardiovascular framework. During the instructional meeting, your pulse is being estimated and showed. Simultaneously a visual and additionally sound pacer is displayed to the student to keep up the explicit beat of relaxing. Utilizing a unique numerical algorithm an impact of paced breathing on heartbeat is being assessed and ceaselessly showed. This algorithm breaks down a degree of consistency between your heart mood and breathing pace at a quite certain pace of around 6 breaths for each moment. The quick impact of such preparing is pressure help and bringing back the body's inward parity. Standard utilization of this method causes different beneficial outcomes, for example, bringing down circulatory strain, reinforcing invulnerable framework, improving absorption, normalizing metabolic procedures, and compound equalization. Everybody manages pressure. It is an awful unavoidable truth for the majority of us; the however there are times when stress can be valuable, for example, when it rouses us to complete things. In any case, very regularly, it tends to be a weight that holds us down, bit by bit transforming into uneasiness, or disturbing existing nervousness issues. With its a wide range of causes, stress is distinctive for each individual, equivalent to uneasiness is. Stress is commonly the ancestor to nervousness assaults, however. Keeping worried under control is probably the ideal approaches to prevent uneasiness from popping up and dominating.

The Connections Between Stress and Anxiety

Anything that makes our minds and bodies respond can be viewed as a sort of stress. At the point when the responses are negative -, for example, quick breathing, perspiring, revived heartbeat, and free guts, among others - is when stress becomes "upsetting" and can start the procedure into gentle nervousness, which has fundamentally similar side effects. Stress alone normally scatters when the stressor is expelled from the circumstance; nervousness doesn't. Uneasiness, when activated by an unpleasant circumstance, can take the ball and continue running, leaving an individual in incredible misery. Contingent upon the nervousness issue present, focusing on variables can be as straightforward as being approached to go to a gathering, to as overwhelming as being compelled to accomplish something that leaves the sufferer in enthusiastic and mental torment. Moreover, stress is some of the time minimal more than having a bustling day that leaves somebody rationally as well as physically depleted, just for them to attempt to return home to their usual range of familiarity and end up stuck in an automobile overload for 60 minutes. For a few, the powerlessness to get away from the pressure of the day in returning home is sufficient to fire uneasiness in working up. Synthetically, stress makes the body discharge cortisol and different hormones, which are utilized to battle stressors and make the vitality to react to them. While this can be great at the hour of introductory pressure, it can likewise cloud the sign going through the piece of the cerebrum, which is additionally firmly liable for uneasiness issues. In this way, it appears that overseeing pressure - not simply outwardly, how we physically respond to it however within, how our body science responds - can be basic in getting synthetic levels back leveled out before they make tension. Strangely, high feelings of anxiety can likewise be connected to misery, substance misuse, mental issue, and various other optional side effects - all of which fall inside the side effects of uneasiness issue, as well. It is anything but difficult to see that the two conditions are firmly related. Contingent upon the nervousness issue, stress can make a repetitive circumstance where stress causes tension, and uneasiness causes more pressure.

Overseeing Stress to Manage Anxiety

So as to oversee uneasiness issue through pressure the executives, it is significant for sufferers to initially comprehend what their tension issue is, and what stress triggers they have. Normally, staying away from these triggers, or slow acclimation to them, is the primary method to prevent worry from causing negative impacts which progress into tension. Obviously, this isn't constantly conceivable in reality, so learning various approaches to deal with these two conditions at the same time is extremely useful.

Primary factors in decreasing and overseeing pressure are physical action and exercise. Getting out from behind the work area, getting up, or off the love, seat to get outside and accomplish something helps, and normally much more than a great many people figure it will. Regardless of whether turning out in a rec center or doing a wellness routine with a DVD before the TV, it will help decrease feelings of anxiety significantly by copying a ton of overabundance synthetic compounds and adrenaline which are simply developing, trusting that something will respond to. Alongside getting some physical exercise, getting, at any rate, thirty minutes worth of daylight daily by being outside (or at any rate approaching windows that let in the regular light) can extraordinarily help diminish pressure and nervousness levels. The individuals who experience the ill effects of high pressure, sorrow or tension should attempt to do their work insufficiently bright regions that permit in common light so as to keep their brains and their bodies the most advantageous.   Different approaches to expand pressure decrease incorporate eating routine and every day propensities. Diet can have an immense impact on overseeing pressure and obviously, tension. Eating a well-adjusted eating regimen that is low in creature fats and high in things like nutrients and lean, solid protein is fundamental for a decent parity of mind synthetic concoctions. Drinking a lot of water keeps up hydration and legitimate cell work. Diminishing caffeine and liquor consumption will in general, help too. Getting enough time for unwinding doing pleasurable things - just as enough rest - is basic, as well. Without sufficient opportunity to allow the body to unwind and energize, it will get exhausted in a steady condition of pressure, which can, in the long run, lead to tension triggers. In the most noticeably awful situations, the drug might be important to help oversee pressure; psychotherapy is strongly suggested when essential, as well. Seeing a specialist in the event that it appears endeavors at the pressure the executives keep on falling flat is exceptionally recommended so as to examine every single accessible choice in assuaging pressure and stopping its continuous stretch into nervousness. Different unwinding methods like contemplation - whenever given the opportunity - can likewise be extraordinary assistance in breaking the cycle among pressure and nervousness, and all their related conditions. Be certain that advancing these endeavors will bring about the important diminished pressure and tension.

Step by step instructions to Deal with Stress and Anxiety

In spite of the fact that the expressions "stress" and "uneasiness" will " in general, be exchangeable in like manner use, restoratively, they are unique. Stress is an ordinary response to a particular danger or circumstance and all things considered; it's anything but confusion. Ordinarily, when the reason is evacuated, the degrees of stress hormones come back to ordinary. Anyway, nervousness is a true blue ailment. All together for tension side effects to be analyzed as a nervousness issue, the manifestations will have persevered for in any event a half year. Tension is one of the potential outcomes of a drawn-out elevated level of pressure, and that goes on without a recognizable reason. Uneasiness is the drawn-out sentiment of dread or dread, maybe without a known reason. The individual harrowed stresses over what lies ahead, and frequently experiences physical indications, for example, alarm assaults, discombobulation. The DSM-IV-TR recognizes these tension issue: fanatical urgent issue (OCD), division uneasiness, youth nervousness issue, explicit fears, alarm issue, alarm issue with agoraphobia, and post-horrendous pressure issue (PTSD). Tension indications can incorporate steady stressing or fixation; it might be over apparently little things or bigger feelings of dread. There might be an inclination of anxiety or general unease, a sentiment of being anxious for no particular reason. There is frequently inconvenience dozing, and sentiment of exhaustion, of being drained significantly following a night's rest. There might be muscle pressure or trembling, which may prompt hurting muscles. Fixation is poor and the mind tends to "go clear." There might be fractiousness, for the most part feeling irascible and horrible. A consistent sentiment of pressure may prompt being effectively frightened, or in any event, trembling. Stomach related bombshell is normal, with loss of craving, or on the other hand looking for desserts, gorging, medications or liquor in the endeavor to feel much improved. Perspiring, queasiness or looseness of the bowels may happen, just as brevity of breath or quick heartbeat. The prior ceaseless pressure and nervousness are tended to, the simpler it is to survive. In any event, by acting rapidly, there is less harm to wellbeing, including brought resistant reaction and harm down to the cardiovascular framework. Comprehensive wellbeing specialists prescribe various techniques to help cut down the feelings of anxiety. Tension issue is an ailment that has continued for some time, and by and large, will adopt an increasingly far-reaching strategy so as to mend.

Careful Meditation and Cognitive Behavioral Therapy
Daniel Smith, who expounded on his battle with tension issues in his book A Monkey Mind, states: "For me, it's care reflection or Cognitive Behavioral Therapy (CBT), which is customized for nervousness." A Boston University study found that uneasiness indications were soothed for individuals who utilized care or Cognitive Behavioral Therapy with the most sensational outcomes being for those with over the top urgent issue and intense pressure issue. The intellectual treatment has been demonstrated to be compelling in assisting with uneasiness issue. Treatment will work best when the individual likewise adds to the procedure by creating solid self-care propensities. Mayo Clinic recommends various way of life programs which will prompt better wellbeing

results. Day by day practice is at the highest priority on the rundown. As indicated by the Anxiety and Depression Association of America, individuals who get standard exercise are 25% less inclined to build up a nervousness issue throughout the following five years.

Stress and Stress Management

Stress is a mental term which implies a disagreeable condition of enthusiastic and physiological excitement that individuals involved with circumstances that they see as hazardous or threatening to their prosperity. The word pressure implies various things to various individuals. A few people characterize worry as occasions or circumstances that reason them to feel the strain, weight, or antagonistic feelings, for example, tension and outrage. Others see worry as the reaction to these circumstances. This reaction incorporates physiological changes, for example, expanded pulse and muscle strain just as passionate and conduct changes. Be that as it may, most analysts see worry as a procedure including an individual's understanding and reaction to a compromising occasion. Stress is a typical encounter. You may feel pressure when you are exceptionally occupied, have significant cutoff times to meet, or have a too brief period to complete every one of your errands. Regularly individuals experience pressure as a result of issues at work or in social connections, for example, a poor assessment by a boss or contention with a companion. A few people might be especially helpless against worry in the circumstances including the danger of disappointment or individual embarrassment. Others have outrageous feelings of dread of items or things related to physical dangers, for example, disease, tempests, or flying in a plane and become pushed when they experience or consider these apparent dangers. Significant life occasions, for example, the demise of a friend or family member, can cause extreme pressure. If not oversaw suitably, stress can prompt genuine medical issues. Introduction to steady pressure can add to both physical ailments, for example, coronary illness, and dysfunctional behaviors, for example, uneasiness issue. The field of wellbeing brain research centers to some degree around how stress influences the real working and on how individuals can utilize pressure the board systems to counteract or limit malady. The conditions that reason pressure are called stressors. Stressors change in seriousness and length. Stressors can be grouped into three general classifications:

- · calamitous occasions
- · significant life changes
- · day by day bothers

Likewise, essentially considering undesirable past occasions or envisioning upsetting future occasions can cause worry for some individuals.

How does Stress influence you?
An individual who is pushed regularly has on edge musings and trouble thinking or recollecting. Stress can likewise change outward practices. Teeth holding, hand

wringing, pacing, nail gnawing, and substantial breathing are regular indications of stress. Individuals likewise feel physically unique when they are pushed. Butterflies in the stomach, cold hands and feet, dry mouth, and expanded pulse are for the most part physiological impacts of pressure that we partner with the feeling of tension.

Ailments

Doctors progressively recognize that pressure is a contributing component in a wide assortment of medical issues. These issues incorporate cardiovascular issues, for example, (hypertension); coronary illness, and gastrointestinal issues, for example, ulcers. Stress likewise seems, by all accounts, to be a hazard factor in malignant growth, ceaseless agony issues, and numerous another wellbeing issue.

Scientists have obviously recognized pressure, and explicitly an individual's trademark method for reacting to worry, as a hazard factor for cardiovascular ailments. The arrival of stress hormones has an aggregate negative impact on the heart and veins.

Stress Management

Adapting to pressure implies utilizing musings and activities to manage unpleasant circumstances and lower your feelings of anxiety. Numerous individuals have a trademark method for adapting to pressure-dependent on their character. Individuals who adapt well to pressure will, in general, accept they can actually impact what befalls them. They, as a rule, own increasingly positive expressions about themselves, oppose disappointment, stay hopeful, and continue on much under incredibly antagonistic conditions. Above all, they pick the fitting systems to adapt to the stressors they face. Alternately, individuals who adapt ineffectively to pressure will, in general, have fairly inverse character attributes, for example, lower confidence and a cynical point of view. Clinicians recognize two wide sorts of adapting techniques: issue centered adapting and feeling centered adapting. The objective of the two systems is to control one's feelings of anxiety. In issue centered adapting, you will attempt to cut off feelings by making some move to alter, maintain a strategic distance from, or limit the undermining circumstance. You should change your conduct to manage the upsetting circumstance. In feeling centered adapting, you should attempt to straightforwardly direct or dispose of upsetting feelings. Instances of feeling centered adapting incorporate reevaluating the circumstance in a positive manner, unwinding, disavowal, and unrealistic reasoning. Notwithstanding that, two other significant strategies for unwinding are dynamic solid unwinding and reflection, which could be exceptionally useful for you. Dynamic, strong unwinding includes efficiently straining and afterward loosening up various gatherings of muscles while coordinating your consideration toward the differentiating sensations delivered by the two systems. Subsequent to rehearsing dynamic solid unwinding, you will turn out to be progressively touchy to rising strain levels and can create the unwinding reaction during regular exercises. Reflection, notwithstanding showing unwinding, is intended to accomplish abstract objectives, for example, examination, intelligence, and adjusted conditions of cognizance. A few structures have a solid Eastern strict and profound legacy situated in Zen Buddhism and yoga. Different assortments underline a specific way of life for professionals. One of the most widely recognized types of reflection, Transcendental Meditation, includes concentrating consideration on and rehashing a mantra, which is a word, sound, or expression thought to have especially quieting properties.

Both dynamic muscle unwinding and reflection dependably decrease pressure-related excitement. They have been utilized effectively to treat a scope of the stress-related issues, including hypertension, headache and pressure cerebral pains, and ceaseless torment.

CHAPTER SEVEN

HOW CBT WORKS?

Intellectual, social treatment (CBT) is an impermanent, objective arranged psychotherapy treatment that takes a hands-on, the functional method for critical thinking. It will probably modify examples of reasoning or conduct which are supporting individuals' issues, thus adjust how they feel. It's utilized to treat a wide grouping of issues in a person's lifetime, from dozing issues or association and medication abuse or stress and despairing. CBT works by changing individuals' demeanors and their conduct by concentrating on the thoughts, pictures, convictions and dispositions which are put away (a person's intellectual methods) and how these procedures identify with how somebody carries on as a method for managing mental issues. A huge advantage of the subjective social treatment is It will be brief, expecting five to ten weeks for some mental issues. Customers go to a solitary session every week, every session enduring around 50 minutes. In this timespan, the customer and advisor will cooperate in comprehending what the issues are and make new approaches for taking care of them. CBT brings patients into some arrangement of standards they can apply each time they need to, and that will last them an actual existence. Intellectual, social treatment is considered as a blend Of psychotherapy and conduct treatment. Psychotherapy underscores the criticalness of the individual centrality we put on things and furthermore how thinking examples start in youth. The restorative treatment gives close consideration to the relationship between our troubles, our conduct and our thoughts. Numerous psychotherapists who practice CBT redo and modify the treatment to the specific needs and character of each person.

The Value of Negative Ideas

CBT depends on a model or idea that it isn't occasioned themselves that steamed us but the hugeness we give them. In the event that our thoughts are excessively negative, it might square us seeing things or doing things which don't coordinate - which disconfirm - that which we believe is precise. To put it in an unexpected way, we keep on continuing to precisely the same old thoughts and don't discover some new information. By Way of Example, a hopeless lady can believe," I cannot stand up to Going into work now: " I cannot do it. Nothing goes right. I will feel horrendous." As a result of these thoughts - and of reasoning them, she could well ring in wiped out. By acting this way, she won't have the chance to discover that her expectation was inaccurate. She may have found a couple of things she can do, and furthermore at certain things which were fine. But instead, she stays at home, agonizing about her inability to continue in and winds up believing:"I have allowed everyone to down. They'll be distraught with me. For what reason cannot I do what every other person does? I am so defenseless and dishonorable." That young lady likely winds up feeling more awful and contains more issues going into work the next day. Figuring, acting and feeling like that may start a descending winding. This endless loop may use many different sorts of issues.

Where Can These Negative Ideas Come From?

Beck showed that these reasoning examples have been set up in Youth, and be programmed and relatively fixed. In this manner, a child who didn't get a lot of open friendship by their folks, however, had been complimented for schoolwork, could come to believe, "I need to do well constantly. In the event that I don't, individuals will decline me" This sort of guideline for a living (called a broken suspicion) can perform pleasantly for the individual a lot of time and license them to work troublesome. In any case, if something happens, that is outside their ability to control and furthermore. They experience disappointment; at that point, the broken idea example may be activated. The individual would then be able to begin to have programmed thoughts enjoy," I have totally dismissed. No one will like me. I cannot go up against them." Intellectual conduct treatment acts to help the

Individual Realize this is what's going on. It causes her or him to step past their programmed thoughts and inspect them out. CBT would advance the hopeless lady referenced before to break down genuine undertakings to discover what befalls her, or others, in comparable situations. Subsequently, at the light of a substantially more sensible point of view, she may be able to choose the plausibility of examining what other people accept, by indicating a portion of her issues to amigos. Unquestionably, negative things can and do happen. Yet, when we're In an agitated outlook, we may be basing our understandings and forecasts onto a one-sided point of view of this condition, which makes the issue that we face look a lot of more regrettable. CBT causes people to fix those misinterpretations.

What Exactly Does CBT Treatment Resemble?

Subjective social treatment contrasts from a Number of Other types Of psychotherapies since journeys have a structure, instead of the individual speaking straightforwardly about whatever rings a bell. Toward the beginning of the treatment, the client meets the advisor to disclose certain troubles and to build up objectives they wish to progress in the direction of. The issues may be irksome side effects, such as dozing inadequately, being not able to associate with companions, or trouble concentrating on contemplating or work environment. Or on the other hand, they are life intricacies, such as being hopeless at work, experiencing issues adapting to a high school youngster, or being in a hopeless marriage. These issues and objectives become the establishment for readiness The material of sessions and examining how to oversee them. For the most part, at the beginning of a session, the customer and advisor may on the whole, pick the primary subjects they wish to work with this week. They'll additionally permit time to talk about the choices from the earlier semester. Furthermore, they'll look at the advancement made with the schoolwork the client set for him or herself last minute. At the end of the session, they'll plan another strategic to perform the sessions.

Doing Homework

Chipping away at schoolwork assignments between sessions, along these lines, is a significant piece of the technique. This may include will change. By method, for example, at the beginning of the treatment, the specialist may request that the client keep up a diary of any scenes that incite sentiments of wretchedness or tension, so they can inspect contemplations encompassing the scene. Later on in the treatment, another crucial incorporate activities to oversee issue circumstances of a particular kind.

The Significance of development

The explanation for having this course of action is that it uses the therapeutic time proficiently. Furthermore, it guarantees that significant data isn't passed up a great opportunity (that the results of the assignments, for instance) and both specialist and customer consider new assignments which clearly pursue on in the session. The specialist takes a functioning part in adjusting the Sessions to begin to. As progress is made, and clients handle the basics they find valuable; they require an expanding number of obligation regarding the substance of sessions. Before the end, the client feels allowed to continue working autonomously.

Gathering sessions

Subjective conduct treatment is generally a balanced treatment. Be that as it may, it's additionally perfect for working in gatherings, or families, particularly at the beginning of treatment. A ton of people discovers advantage from examining their issues together with others who may have comparative challenges, regardless of the way this may appear to be overwhelming at first. The group may likewise be a wellspring of especially important help and direction since it originates from people with individual experience of an issue. Moreover, by observing various individuals simultaneously, specialist co-ops can give assistance to more people accurately precisely the same time, so people get help prior.

What other means does this vary from different medications?

Psychological, social treatment contrasts from different Therapies in the pith of the association the advisor will endeavor to set up. A few medicines encourage the purchaser to be controlled by the advisor inside the treatment strategy. The client can then promptly come to see the specialist as all-knowing and all-incredible. The association contrasts with CBT. CBT favors an increasingly equivalent relationship, which is, perhaps, more Business-like, being issue engaged just as useful. The specialist will regularly approach the client for remarks and for their points of view about what's going on in treatment. Beck begat the term'collaborative induction', which features the hugeness of specialist and customer cooperating to evaluate how the ideas behind CBT may apply to the client's individual circumstance and issues.

Specialists and Disadvantages of Cognitive Behavior

Therapy

Psychological, social treatment (CBT) gives a blend of conduct and talk treatment to help individuals reframe their negative reasoning examples. The goal of CBT is to transform those negative examples into positive thoughts. In the event that this adjustment in context is cultivated, at that point, positive practices and exercises convey what needs be through troublesome minutes or alternatives in such a person's reality. A few issues influence people Every Day, from detachment to Stress to sorrow. Each individual looks for comfort during those occasions inside their own way. A few choices may prompt destructive practices, while a few, for example, a dietary problem, can cause long haul medical problems whenever left untreated.

All through a CBT session, a patient capacities with their advisor to find the root of the negative reasoning. They at that point work to adjust this viewpoint toward a development based outlook. With adequate time, numerous people may discover ways of dealing with stress that is sound, letting them perceive the thoughts, feelings, and practices that keep them down. These are the Substantial Advantages and Disadvantages of intellectual Behavioral treatment to reassess.

Rundown of the Experts of Cognitive Behavior Therapy

1. it's as compelling as medication to treat some mental wellbeing afflictions. Around 7 percent of grown-ups in the USA experience the ill effects of a noteworthy burdensome issue each year. The pointers of the medical issue remember a decrease of enthusiasm for things recently appreciated, lower vitality levels, physical issue development, and seclusion. Serious issues with critical burdensome issue may get perilous if not treated. When CBD is pursued intently, the negative idea designs have been revamped, which can help assuage moderate examples when under the consideration of a specialist as successfully as medication does.

2. CBT doesn't require a lot of time to complete

contrasted with various types of talking treatment. Patients that experience psychological, social treatment will normally meet to get an Individual session that goes on for 30 minutes, circumventing an hour, Based upon the issues in question. You would meet with your specialist about once per week or once every other week, contingent upon the situation involved. People that Receive presentation treatment, for the most part, have more sessions that are broadened. Numerous CBT show keeps going for 2keepsnths or not. A few patients Complete utilizing their subjective conduct treatment in just five weeks. In contrast with other garrulous cures that may suffer for quite a long time, or become a consistent treatment help, CBT licenses you to experience results straight away.

3. The consideration of CBT takes on various arrangements, Based upon the subjects introducing themselves. Issues are partitioned into five head territories inside intellectual, social treatment: situations, thoughts, feelings, real emotions, and

exercises. The goal of the sessions will be to uncover patients that these sections are associated with each other in the brain. In the event that you stand up to a difficult circumstance, at that point, you have an idea created out of it. That thought leads to a feeling. The feeling adds to the physical appearance of these sentiments. At that point, the articulations cause activities or choices. CBT makes opportunities to take on various configurations of Expression as indicated by where the mistakes happen in a person's life. Introduction treatment manages headaches and over the top enthusiastic sickness. Patients may recognize negative idea cycles. Regardless of your present issues are, you are going to investigate how you accepted and acted before to change what you would do later on.

4. Distinctive treatment session instruments and types are Accessible through CBT. The garrulous treatment has become the most successive intends to begin connecting with intellectual, social treatment. There are various apparatuses accessible for people to utilize while attempting to rebuild their reasoning examples

too. It is conceivable to peruse books that discussion about the points that you accept are imperative to your current needs. You can discover bunch sessions utilized once in a while to assist you with understanding that you're not the only one. Recordings, PC applications, and even road trips are sometimes included as treatment decisions. That is on the grounds that the goal is to help you work in manners that vibe agreeable and normal to you.

5. The aptitudes learned through each CBT session. Offer valuable genuine capacities. At the point when you are working with a conduct treatment advisor, what you're doing would be expertise based practice. You're recognizing adapting methodologies that might be used in practically any situation you end up. By discovering approaches to manage pressure and uneasiness, the outcomes that it gets become less incredible in your lifetime. You become stronger because of that activity, gaining positive cycles that energize ground toward a cure. This recognizable proof of managing expertise mechanics makes it possible

that you deal with ceaseless self-antagonism, high-stress environment, or difficult circumstances since you know the bigger picture through CBT. You are not any more caught in the outrageous thoughts, emotions, and practices that get activated by the undesirable incitement.

6. CBT is a collective work. When going through subjective conduct treatment, your specialist isn't probably going to tell you precisely what to do. They cooperate with you rather get an answer to the issues you face at the present time. This typically implies you distinguish issues on an individual level; at that point, put resources into yourself to make the modifications that are vital. It's this system that becomes valuable when reacting to different situations. Since CBT is a cooperative undertaking, there's More Accountability into the technique. At whatever point you have a life partner, you are essentially bound to discover achievement.

7. Medication can utilize intellectual conduct treatment. CBT is certainly not a treatment elective

which must be utilized alone. Numerous doctors prescribe psychological, social treatment when drug alone isn't working. A few people today endure with over a substance irregularity utilizing their enthusiastic medical problems. Their reasoning examples become horrible through outside incitement, for example, their home condition, which no medications could contact. The accomplishment pace of medication and CBT is enormous in numerous socioeconomics, offering a sensible course of plan to overcome this hindrance for some.

8. CBT is helpful for all intents and purposes of any age gathering. Children and grown-ups advantage from subjective social treatment when appropriately utilized. The desires will be precisely the same in any age classification. Given that there's a potential and will to make changes in your lifetime, at that point, CBT gives an answer which may see to the issues which exist. In any event, accepting the open the door to talk about a condition is adequate to supply a few outcomes in light of the fact that a ton of people keep

predicament disguised, which makes them putrefy since they don't examine their interests with others.

CBT is an approach to create trust in oneself as well as other people while Working to break antagonistic cycles and their destructive impacts throughout everyday life. The probability of finishing an objective when you are liable to somebody for it's 95%. In the event that you essentially know about intellectual, social treatment and that is up to the treatment thought broadens, at that point your chances of achievement drops to just 10%.

Rundown of those Disadvantages of Cognitive Behavior Therapy

1. Psychological conduct treatment depends on the desire Of the person. Each individual must be spent in themselves to get psychological, social treatment to carry out the responsibility. Through the treatment session, you will be gotten some information about what you hope to pick up in the activity you are doing.

You need to inspect the urges, causes, and headaches that reason you trouble. The advisor may hear your interests; anyway it's everything up to you to put in the activity that must be done so as to make a change. In the event that you are hesitant to assemble a technique or work on Prep for another semester, at that point, the results of your CBT experience will get restricted. Everyone taking part in intellectual conduct treatment needs to completely help out the strategy to make benefits.

2. It Requires a Whole Lot of time to complete CBT with the Additional work between sessions. Schoolwork is possibly the most significant piece of intellectual, social treatment. The missions you will wrap up your opportunity in CBT arrive out of development including the advisor helping you. Most of the work requests request the practice of new capacities working on during a treatment session. Adapting procedures are polished and grew likewise, together with time spent at the rebuilding of hurtful conviction frameworks. I hope to spend at any rate 1-2

hours every day chipping away at those Curative components. A few people may need to twofold their time commitment. Every semester requires finished missions are the most helpful, so a great deal of your spare time might be gotten from your subjective social treatment obligations.

3. CBT Isn't Helpful for individuals with specific learning issues. Experiential treatment is the chief configuration that subjective social treatment uses to treat individuals with specific learning issues. By taking a hands-on methodology, the intellectual challenges looked by the individual included are defeated through the piece of genuine practice. This system doesn't work for everyone, however, since it depends on a domain viewed as secure by the individual. There are a couple of learning issues which evacuate all sheltered environment, confining the implications CBT makes.

4. People with complex emotional well-being needs probably won't profit by CBT either. Subjective social treatment attempts to rebuild issues, for example, worry by modifying how thoughts are prepared. With

muddled fears or mental medical problems, CBT isn't valuable as there are specific components of threat that continually utilize at times. Require someone who fears flying, for example. Somebody is statistically more secure flying than driving, anyway when a plane drops from 30,000 ft and accidents, you are 100% dead. A few people today meander away from rapid head-on crashes. You might be factually more secure in a plane, however, when an episode occurs, the individual with the fear would state they are measurably more secure at the vehicle. Turning out to be psychological with respect to thoughts isn't really an assurance in which advances are made.

5. Subjective conduct treatment, as often as possible, exacerbates individuals' feel before they feel good. CBT needs individuals to confront the issues which make troublesome affections for them. During the principal sessions and assignments finished by the individual, the main encounter of dread, apprehension, or different challenges creates a spike in negative thoughts and emotions. It's not unusual for physical

exercises to turn out to be more awful too. Someone who battles with forlornness and arrangements by ingesting may end up as often as possible checking the cooler for a nibble in this period. The outcomes of subjective social treatment Start to uncover Themselves following the initial a few sessions and the related assignments. On the off chance that an individual chooses to stop during the main stage when side effects will, in general, be more regrettable, it may put the person at a circumstance that is more defenseless than beforehand.

6. CBT addresses present issues just as opposed to addressing some characteristic causes. The goal of intellectual, social treatment is to deal with issues that go up against a person right now. That point of view endeavors to break the person from the pessimistic accepting cycles, rebuilding their thoughts toward something constructive. There are cases, however, when ceaseless issues make negative cycles and CBT doesn't, generally deal with the issue. Have a young loaded with steady travel and movement. A while later,

a parent leaves the family unit at a young age, catching the person at a cycle of destitution before their immature years. They battle with over the top habitual issues on the grounds that everything holds worth to them. They can't release things as they're genuinely connected to each item. Surveying the connection through psychological conduct treatment won't change how the individual arrangements with the parent that deserted them which might be the heart issue driving the negative cycles in the primary area.

7. It focuses on the individual ability to change. People must be set up to adjust for subjective conduct treatment to work appropriately. There likewise must be a solitary capacity to change for CBT to give helpful results. On the off chance that an individual is encouraged to utilize a PC programming as a major aspect of the treatment, however they don't approach this innovation, at that point it won't be a reasonable interest. The apparatuses upheld for assignments, group sessions, or 1-on-1 treatment must offer openness to the person for thought rebuilding to

occur. Nothing happens with no entrance.

The Advantages and Disadvantages of intellectual social treatment work to Find valuable methodologies to react to circumstances instead of depending on unhelpful techniques. As opposed to tolerating that you're a disappointment because of what strikes you, caught in a negative propensity, CBT persuades you to begin searching for positive potential. It makes your issues increasingly sensible, despite the fact that there are circumstances when it probably won't be the correct helpful decision to pick.

CHAPTER EIGHT

ADHD AND PSYCHOLOGICAL DISORDERS

ADHD, what is it precisely? Consideration Deficit Hyperactivity Disorder is a formative issue typically causing carelessness, distractibility, impulsivity, and hyperactivity in kids beginning before the age of seven. ADHD is an interminable issue that happens in 3-5% of kids around the world. The contention encompassing ADHD has been around since the '70s. A few people don't accept that ADHD is a real issue; others trust it has a hereditary or physiological premise. Significantly more debate encompasses the treatment for ADHD. Medicines incorporate conduct alterations, way of life changes, advising and energizer drug.

Presently days whenever a kid is hyper guardians think it is ADHD. Between 2-16% of children in school are determined to have ADHD and given a prescription for this issue. Numerous children, anyway, are typically misdiagnosed. Numerous manifestations of ADHD can be credited to a different issues, huge numbers of which can go with ADHD. Since such mixes of disarranges show up together, this can convolute determination. There are five social manifestations that have been credited to ADHD, however, are really not side effects of ADHD legitimately. Huge numbers of these indications are misdiagnosed as ADHD when in fact they are their very own issue and ought to be treated in that capacity. The five issues are Anxiety, melancholy, problematic conduct, learning incapacities, and tangible coordination issue.

1. Nervousness is a mental and physiological state described by sentiments of stress, anxiety, and dread. Uneasiness can be activated by an individual, a spot, or even an inclination. The upgrade can even be unidentifiable apparently to others. It's harder to analyze kids that have nervousness to a great extent because of the way that children articulate their emotions considerably less than grown-ups do. Children with nervousness generally seem engrossed or daydreamed. This is because of their interior

considerations of stress. Children with nervousness don't have a clue how to deal with or express their uneasiness and see their dangers as wild and unavoidable.

2. Despondency is a state of mind issue described by sentiments of misery, weakness, and sadness that can bring about an antipathy for action. Sorrow can impede thinking abilities, memory, psychological adaptability, and consideration. Individuals who experience the ill effects of wretchedness typically appear to be out of it. They experience difficulty centering, become bad-tempered, and have an absence of intrigue or inception. Wretchedness has nobody single reason. Family ancestry, cynical character, injury and stress, physical conditions, and other mental issues would all be able to be related to discouragement. For other people, sorrow had no explicit trigger or cause. Since youngsters have more trouble communicating their feelings, it's imperative to decide sadness in kids through the assessment of the kid's conduct in a few settings.

3. Problematic Behavior is the place a youngster won't settle down and gets inconvenient or jumbled. Particularly in a school setting, this can turn into an issue where the problematic understudy doesn't enable different understudies to learn. At times children can be troublesome purposefully, to flaunt, be amusing or look cool. Anyway, kids that have problematic practices, as a rule, feel baffled and are defying power to bring consideration upon them. These kinds of children have not created satisfactory restraint, which makes them carry on and at last reason interruptions for different colleagues.

4. Learning incapacities is a characterization of scatters where an individual experiences issues learning. These disarrange have influenced the cerebrum's capacity to get and process data in this way making it horribly hard for the individual to learn. Since we don't have the foggiest idea what causes this issue inside the mind learning inabilities are difficult to fix. Be that as it may, there are different approaches to get around learning inabilities. Intercession and backing are the most

significant alternatives accessible to somebody who has a learning handicap. Learning inabilities in kids can cause mindlessness, troublesome conduct, tension and sorrow. There are many learning inabilities, for example, perusing, composing, math issue, visual discernment, sound-related preparing, nonverbal, dyslexia and so on.

5. Tactile Integration Disorder (SID) is a neurological issue where the individual can't arrange tangible data as it gets through the faculties. At the point when present in a youngster, the kid may seem careless or an incredible inverse as hyperactive. This is brought about by the kid being oversensitive or under delicate to the tangible upgrades encompassing him/her. A youngster with a tangible joining issue might be upset by uproarious commotions, brilliant lights, unpleasant surfaces, or smells; or alternately, may need to deal with things, hang topsy turvy, or yell riotously. As should be obvious from the depictions of everyone of these clutters, huge numbers of the side effects are the

equivalent or fundamentally the same as. A significant number of these disarranges go with one another and in this way, the individual might be managing a few distinct issues simultaneously. Since a considerable lot of these disarranges are currently influencing youngsters also it's imperative to assess and analyze appropriately. Along these lines, we can appropriately treat for the right issue and stop over-curing of our youngsters, which can cause them to hurt in their future.

Different Bipolar Disorder Symptoms and Treatments
Everybody lives with new difficulties every day, which may influence the sort of individual they become. A few people endure enough that they are persuaded there is no reason for proceeding with life. In some cases, the purpose behind this grim viewpoint originates from a mental issue, for example, bipolar. A great many people who have bipolar conditions realize that this will have a significant effect in their day by day life. This sort of turmoil creates in the late pre-adulthood or early adulthood. Be that as it may, there

are additionally youngsters that have been recognized as having it. Bipolar issue is the offered name to depict a lot of 'emotional episode' conditions that is felt by an individual. Its most serious type is called 'hyper discouragement'. This issue may influence both genders. Be that as it may, ladies who have it will, for the most part, have more scenes of sadness, while men are progressively inclined in the first place hyper scenes. Specialists expressed that the confusion has no single reason. It has been indicated that a few people are hereditarily inclined to it. In any case, not every person with a genetic obligation creates it. We should observe that not just qualities cause it. It additionally accepted that outside conditions and mental components are associated with building up the ailment. The bipolar issue is partitioned into a few sorts and every ha various examples of side effects. These include: bipolar I, bipolar II, cyclothymia, fast cycling, and blended bipolar. Bipolar I issue is a more extreme issue. Individuals with type I experience longer 'highs' and have maniacal encounters while the individuals who are experiencing bipolar II issues have less serious manifestations. They experienced scenes that lone an hour ago or hardly any days and the seriousness of the 'highs' doesn't prompt hospitalization. Cyclothymia is a gentle type of confusion. The individuals who have cyclothymia will, in general, have more mellow indications than without and out bipolar issues. About 10% of individuals with the bipolar disease have fast cycling. In quick cycling, at least four scenes of despondency in a year happen. In many types of bipolar conditions, states of mind fluctuate among raised and discouraged yet with the blended bipolar issues, an individual encounters both madness and melancholy all the while. Each kind of bipolar issue may influence various individuals in an unexpected way. The manifestations differ in example and seriousness. The confusion was generally alluded to as a piece of sorrow; however, specialists prescribe that there are critical contrasts among discouragement and bipolar indications. Side effects of bipolar issues can ruin occupation and school execution, ruin your associations with friends and family and disturb day by day life. Albeit bipolar is treatable, numerous individuals don't perceive the side effects and should realize that it will, in general, intensify without treatment. In this manner it is basic to know the side effects and to have the best possible treatment. The initial step to diminish bipolar issues is to get familiar with the turmoil and perceive those who are encountering it. A few specialists prescribed that medicine can anticipate scenes yet more changed treatment can be superior to drugs. Medicine alone isn't sufficient to completely control the sickness. Bipolar requires long haul treatment since it is a constant ailment. Study shows that on the off chance that you are free from pressure and keep up a solid work-life balance, you are more averse to endure. The vast majority of all, encircle yourself with companions that you can go to, who will help and empower you. A specialist can likewise help discover a path between the turns and turns that you feel. Self-destructive contemplations and conduct are normal among individuals with the bipolar issues. To dispose of these contemplations, first, contact a relative or your friends and family and look for help from your primary care physicians. The best treatment procedure for bipolar treatment includes a blend of medicine, treatment and a way of life change. The objective of treatment is to recuperate from the more drawn out disturbances of life. Managing bipolar issue isn't simple yet to have a fruitful treatment; you need to settle on brilliant decisions. On the off chance that you disregard the disease, it will unquestionably deteriorate. Living with the untreated bipolar issue can prompt issues in relations and vocation. Antidepressants don't help individuals with the confusion in the long haul. Indeed, they may considerably trigger quick cycling between states of mind. On the off chance that you feel vulnerable and sad you ought to recollect that you are not the only one.

The most effective method to choose the Best Treatment For Anxiety Disorders

Uneasiness issue is a term used to incorporate a few other explicit issues related to stress, dread, pressure and nervousness. Fears or nonsensical feelings of dread are instances of a nervousness issue. An individual experiencing alarm assaults or frenzy issue is additionally considered as having a tension issue and is encouraged to look for treatment. There are various side effects that can decide if an individual has the confusion or not. Be that as it may, not these indications can be found in one individual. Exorbitant perspiring, palpitation, expanded weariness, cerebral pains, and focus issues are instances of these manifestations. Uneasiness issues are regularly considered because of the amassing of pressure, weakness and injury. The tension assault debilitates the resistant framework and the spirit of the influenced person. Cautious and normal observing of the individual encountering the confusion is positively fundamental.

Uneasiness issues are additionally firmly connected to minor or significant despondency and other related mental issue. A wide assortment of elements are viewed as potential triggers of the disarranges. These particular causes or factors may likewise be pertinent to other mental issues. Nervousness issue can be activated by any outside boosts, for example, any items or any individual. An individual encountering issue may feel outrageous nervousness and dread with an unbiased boost, for example, a vehicle or pencil. Each time the individual sees a vehicle or a pencil, a tension assault occurs, as shown by its side effects. It would be extremely useful if activating improvement can be recognized. This should be possible through the perception of the influenced person. The initial phase in treating tension issue is counseling or looking for a proficient help from therapists or specialists. An analyst or a specialist can recognize how serious the turmoil is and what specific methodology would be material. Treatments for people encountering scatters are centered around beating the nervousness and dread related to a specific boost. Treatments are regularly grouped into intellectual or conduct. The uneasiness assault is regularly viewed as brought about by pervasive contemplations. These common musings would be revealed through intellectual treatment. Likewise, a tension assault additionally triggers occasions that further lead to explicit conduct responses from the individual encountering the turmoil. These conduct responses are distinguished through social methodologies. A few meds may likewise be useful in treating the issue. Notwithstanding, the reactions of these drugs can't likewise be denied. Despite the fact that their symptoms are for the most part, minor, some reactions may likewise carry major unsafe impacts on the person. An individual with a turmoil is frequently encouraged to take meds for a year. On the off chance that there has been a critical improvement, the drug admission can be halted however, on the off chance that there is none, the dose is typically expanded. A few people who used to take prescriptions for the confusion additionally report repeat of tension assaults and other pessimistic social signs after they quit taking drugs. Along these lines, some of them would wind up being excessively reliant and oppressive of the medication. Prescriptions are then considered as a subsequent option with regards to treatment for tension issues. Consideration shortage/hyperactivity issue (ADHD) is one of the most well-known mental issues influencing youngsters. ADHD additionally influences numerous grown-ups. Side effects of ADHD incorporate obliviousness (not having the option to keep center), hyperactivity (abundance development that isn't fitting to the setting) and impulsivity (hurried acts that happen at the time without thought). An expected 8.4 percent of youngsters and 2.5 percent of grown-ups have ADHD.1,2 ADHD is frequently first distinguished in school-matured kids when it prompts disturbance in the homeroom or issues with homework. It can likewise influence grown-ups. It is more typical among young men than young ladies.

Indications and Diagnosis

Numerous ADHD indications, for example, high activity levels, trouble staying still for extensive stretches of time and constrained abilities to focus, are basic to small kids when all is said in done. The distinction in youngsters with ADHD is that their hyperactivity and carelessness are observably more prominent than anticipated for their age and cause trouble as well as issues working at home, at school or with companions. ADHD is analyzed as one of three sorts: unmindful sort, hyperactive/imprudent sort, or consolidated sort. A finding depends on the side effects that have happened in the course of recent months.

Scatterbrained sort – six (or five for individuals more than 17 years) of the accompanying side effects happen as often as possible:

Doesn't give close consideration to subtleties or commits imprudent errors in school or employment assignments.

Has issues remaining concentrated on errands or

exercises, for example, during talks, discussions, or long perusing.

Doesn't appear to listen when addressed (i.e., is by all accounts somewhere else).

Doesn't adhere to through on guidelines and doesn't finish homework, errands, or occupation obligations (may begin assignments yet rapidly loses center).

Has issues arranging errands and work (for example, doesn't oversee time well; has untidy, disrupted work; misses cutoff times).

Maintains a strategic distance from or despises assignments that require continued mental exertion, for example, getting ready reports and finishing structures.

Regularly loses things required for undertakings or everyday life, for example, school papers, books, keys, wallets, PDA and eyeglasses.

Is effectively occupied.

Overlooks day by day undertakings, for example, doing tasks and getting things done. More seasoned adolescents and grown-ups may neglect to return telephone calls, take care of tabs, and keep arrangements.

Hyperactive/indiscreet sort – six (or five for individuals more than 17 years) of the accompanying manifestations happen often:

Squirms with or taps hands or feet or squirms in seat.

Not ready to remain situated (in homeroom, working environment).

Runs about or climbs where it is wrong.

Incapable of playing or doing recreation exercises unobtrusively.

Continuously "in a hurry," as though determined by an engine.

Blabbers.

Proclaims an answer before an inquiry has been made (for example, may complete individuals' sentences, can hardly wait to talk in discussions).

Experiences issues holding up their turn, for example, while holding up in line.

Hinders or interrupts others (for example, cuts into discussions, games, or exercises, or starts utilizing others' things without authorization). More established teenagers and grown-ups may assume control over what others are doing.

There is no lab test to analyze ADHD. The analysis includes gathering data from guardians, instructors and others, rounding out agendas and having a restorative assessment (counting vision and hearing screening) to preclude other therapeutic issues. The indications are not the aftereffect of an individual being rebellious or threatening or unfit to comprehend an errand or directions.

The Causes of ADHD

Researchers have not yet distinguished the particular reasons for ADHD. There is proof that hereditary qualities add to ADHD. For instance, three out of four kids with ADHD have a relative with the turmoil. Different elements that may add to the advancement of ADHD incorporate being conceived rashly, mind damage, and the mother smoking, utilizing liquor or having outrageous worry during pregnancy.

Treatment

ADHD and the School-Aged Child

Educators and school staff can give guardians and specialists data to help assess conduct and learning issues and can help with social preparing. Notwithstanding, school staff can't analyze ADHD, settle on choices about treatment or necessitate that an understudy takes a drug to go to class. Just guardians and watchmen can settle on those choices with the kid's doctor. Understudies whose ADHD debilitates their learning may fit the bill for a custom curriculum under the Individuals with Disabilities Education Act or for a Section 504 arrangement (for kids who don't require specialized curriculum) under the Rehabilitation Act of 1973. Kids with ADHD can profit by study abilities guidance, changes to the homeroom arrangement, elective showing methods, and an adjusted educational plan.

ADHD and Adults

Numerous grown-ups with ADHD don't understand they have the turmoil. An exhaustive assessment normally incorporates an audit of past and current side effects, a medicinal test and history, and utilization of grown-up rating scales or agendas. Grown-ups with ADHD are treated with medicine, psychotherapy, or a blend. Conduct the executive's systems, for example, approaches to limit interruptions and increment structure and association, and including close relatives, can likewise be useful.

Over the top nervousness and a lot of stress are regularly brought about by too elevated standards or inaccessible objectives. Stress established from issues on defining too significant standards or desires may happen in days or a while to a great extent relying upon how the individual can control wretchedness and nervousness. The person with a general tension issue may discover trouble controlling the progression of considerations and compelling feelings. The sign of general tension issues is unreasonable and wild stress. You have to figure out how to control your feelings as a feature of your enemy of maturing care.

Summed up Anxiety Disorder

Summed up nervousness issue happens when you can't control your feelings and your considerations and keep on feeling stressed on specific occasions, which could step by step worry you, have a few types of fits of anxiety and make you feel terrified of specific things that may occur later on. Any individual interfacing with his quick condition could get summed up uneasiness condition paying little heed to age. You may have seen that GAD, for the most part, influences any person's psychological well-being and individual connections. Any individual, kid, or grown-up, may encounter GAD. Along these lines, expect that even your youngster who is only 7 or 8 years of age, could build up the tension issue during his everyday companion association. Any youngster has the most noteworthy likelihood to encounter alarm assaults whenever in his youth from dread, harasser effects, or gathering social weight. Be that as it may, ladies are twice liable to build up the fit of anxiety issues than men. The issue may vary based on recurrence, force, and span. This condition may meddle with the person's ordinary working since it frequently goes with physiological side effects.

The most effective method to Diagnose and Treat Anxiety Condition or Depression for your Anti Aging Care

Summed up, uneasiness condition is an ailment that

could make some type of passionate and mental aggravation without the event of fits of anxiety. A few examinations pronounced that the interrelationship of indications among discouragement and tension is noteworthy. Stray or general nervousness issue covers the condition for melancholy, which is frequently portrayed by wild stress and tension over a wide scope of concerns. Tension and stress are unmistakable highlights or causal factors in creating different types of mental issues, for example, dietary issues or fits of anxiety.

Manifestations of general nervousness issue

• Fixation issues

• Incapable to rest soundly

• Anxiety

• can't eat well

• Less tolerance

• Muscle strain

Individuals encountering general tension condition or despondency likewise experience negative emotionality. Be that as it may, a great many people who have momentary tension can keep up constructive feelings without misery. An individual encountering uneasiness ordinarily experiences discombobulation, breathing trouble, quicker heartbeat, and feeling unstable legs. Comorbidity of uneasiness issue is regular to person. The nearness of at least one issue alludes as comorbidity, where an individual could encounter nervousness and simultaneously experience gloom that in many cases, share similar vulnerabilities of conceivably forming into a fit of anxiety.

Physical conditions brought by tension and sadness

Tension issues can initiate other physical conditions, for example, thyroid ailment, joint pain, unfavorably susceptible conditions, headache, migraines, respiratory malady, and gastrointestinal infection. Individuals could start with the tension issue and wind up having various physical conditions however not a mental issues. This would mean controlling uneasiness is basic to keeping up the general prosperity of a person. The downturn manifestations are inescapable.

A Treatment for Panic Disorder That Really Works

Numerous individuals experience the ill effects of uneasiness and frenzy. It is an incredibly startling encounter for anybody experiencing such confusion. Unwarranted feelings of trepidation, for example, having a coronary failure, not having the option to breathe or gagging to death, may show a frenzy issue. The individuals who have ever endured an assault realize exactly how handicapping and alarming they can be. Luckily, there is currently a basic treatment for those that might be experiencing this incapacitating issue. This issue can be achieved because of the individual experiencing tension or fits of anxiety. This might be brought about by different pressure issues present in sufferer's life. It can likewise be expedited by outrageous feelings of trepidation and dangers to one's very own mortality. It isn't simply a question of feeling your apprehensions and strolling through your dread, on the grounds that numerous sufferers can't start to make a move when stood up to with an assault that perseveres through such serious sentiments.

There is a treatment that doesn't include unwinding, positive assertions, entrancing, or NLP. It is one straightforward technique to prevent your frenzy from grabbing hold of your body and transforming it into shuddering chaos. This strategy is a progressed intellectual procedure that takes standards of brain research and applies them to your condition. It is useful to people experiencing these assaults and you will feel alleviation very quickly from following the means laid out in the program. Those experiencing Generalized Anxiety Disorder or fits of anxiety should have confidence they are not experiencing a medicinal sickness or mental issue. They are basically misconstruing their body's response to push. Their body is going into a battle or flight mode in response to straightforward ordinary boosts. Many frenzy sufferers have discovered that there is a characteristic that does it without anyone's help treatment accessible that can assist them with ending their frenzy issue for the last time. It may not be in a split second, yet not long after starting to pursue the means they have broken free of their frenzy issue, and you can as well. Treatment for alarm issue is just a couple of snaps away. Intellectual Behavioral Therapy is a useful treatment for alarm issues since it manages to uncover the apprehensions and causes you to stroll through the related dread. This treatment joins learning unwinding strategies to help you to discard the dread. There are different alternatives accessible for treating the turmoil. Psychodynamic treatment looks at the inner battles you might be encountering which incite nervousness and dread. It focuses on making you acquainted with your inner conflicts. When you are exposing the battles which are causing the scenes, you can bargain on them successfully. Contemplation treatment is benefited as a characteristic treatment. It causes you to focus on your breathing and encourages you to unwind. It is truly important on the grounds that you can perform it at whatever point you experience the sentiment of an assault going ahead.

Every one of these treatments is demonstrated to be fruitful in treating the confusion. Your specialist or specialist will assist you with choosing which one of the medicines will work best for your concern.

People who are battling to discover a treatment for alarm issue can discover an answer and feel that their life is significantly more sensible in such a little league outline utilizing this straightforward method. Numerous audits of this program have been done, and it has been seen as a genuine program that offers genuine advantages.

Most Common Anxiety Disorder Symptoms

Uneasiness issue is portrayed by a strange dread and overstated nervousness over various parts of regular daily existence without strong and clear motivations to get stressed. Individuals who have nervousness conditions can't help themselves from agonizing a lot over cash, relationship, work, family, wellbeing, and school. The lives of individuals who are experiencing it are ruled by unreasonable dread, fear and tension with the end goal that their perspectives and level of working in a school, working environment and the family unit are fundamentally influenced. Individuals who have nervousness issues regularly have the dread of kicking the bucket, a dread of losing control and dread of approaching fate. They are increasingly hesitant and they fear to submit botches. They would prefer even not to be in broad daylight puts constantly. They have fears of being caught and they continually feel overpowered. Mind science, hereditary qualities, and condition factors are viewed as the primary supporters in the improvement of this issue. This mental issue is typically portrayed by various side effects, for example, over the top and ongoing pressure or stress, unreasonable and adjusted perspective on issues, eagerness, the sentiment of being 'restless,' crabbiness, muscle strain and cerebral pain. Individuals who are experiencing tension issues additionally will in general, experience trouble in concentrating, visit need to go the solace room, tiredness, getting frightened effectively and experience difficulty in falling and staying unconscious particularly during the night. The one of a kind hereditary and individuals additionally will, in general, create unfavorably susceptible responses to various allergens. They additionally experience back agony, fits, firmness, weight, irritation and stability of the back muscles.

There are likewise situations where the sufferer feels a consuming, bothersome, thorny, and extreme sensation on the skin. At some point, they feel peculiar, odd or outside towards everything around them. Weariness, constant exhaustion, ungainliness and poor coordination of body appendages are bound to show up in individuals with tension issues. Others additionally will in general, experience debilitating of the muscles, arms and legs with shivering sensations in various pieces of the body. A portion of the exploited people feels that the floor and the roof are moving for reasons unknown by any means. There are considerably different other people who wake up in the center of the night lavishly perspiring and have a compelling impulse to pee. A low degree of vitality and lack of engagement towards sexual exercises may likewise show. The most widely recognized side effects of tension issues are trembling, tremors and shaking. There are likewise quick palpitations of the heart and muscles will in general, vibrate, tremor, jitter and shake when they are utilized. Sickness, heaving and shooting torments in various pieces of the body, for example, head, face, neck, scalp and back, tenacious muscle strains, throbbing of the muscles and deadness can now and again be normal for individuals who have uneasiness issue. The appearance of a portion of the side effects referenced above doesn't imply that an individual has an uneasiness issue. Yet, when bunches of the indications referenced are seen as famous and present in an individual, it is ideal to counsel restorative experts for right and appropriate findings. Along these lines, prompt medicines will be utilized before the mental condition gets most noticeably awful.

Disposing of Psychological Disorders and Finding Sound Mental Health

The logical technique for dream translation will promptly give you support. Dream treatment is an ensured treatment that will doubtlessly assist you with discovering sound emotional wellness, taking out any mental issue and psychological sicknesses that are causing enduring. Carl Jung's disclosures concerning the importance of dreams give new answers to the world. I proceeded with his examination and streamlined his troublesome strategy. Presently, normal individuals can discover harmony and bliss by contemplating the logical strategy for dream understanding utilizing my improvement. They can approach this information on the web. They can likewise legitimately present their fantasies to me for an expert dream interpretation. Your fantasies are spoken to in representative structure. They work like cautions that shield your emotional well-being from the assaults of the counter inner voice, the wild side of your heart. Your wild inner voice didn't advance. It is a foolish and shrewdness creature that can think. Its considerations depend on madness since it didn't figure out how to locate a mental equalization. Your fantasies are reports that assist you with counteracting the pulverization of your human still, small voice by the counter still, small voice. They normally reflect hazardous circumstances; in light of the fact that the oblivious personality that delivers your fantasies, shows you in an emblematic structure, what the counter soul is doing against your human still, small voice. You overlook the substance of your wild still, small voice. Notwithstanding, the counter soul can peruse your musings and meddle with them. The counter heart can think consistently; however it pursues the ludicrous rationale of narrow-mindedness. You don't have the foggiest idea about that not every one of the contemplations that cross your thoughts has a place with your human heart. Some of them originate from your ridiculous wild still, small voice; however they show up in your brain as though they were 'your own musings.' The counter inner voice is a dubious fiend that professes to be you so as to obliterate your human still, small voice through the madness. It needs to control your conduct as opposed to being restrained by your human reasonableness and affectability. Your fantasies have a baffling and risky viewpoint since they mirror the perilous fight existing between your human still, small voice, and your wild heart. You will wipe out your mental issue by killing the noxious impact of the counter still, small voice in your contemplations and conduct. The counter inner voice figures out how to control your conduct when you concur with its ridiculous proposals. The savvy oblivious personality tells you in dream messages the best way to see its impact. Through dream interpretation, you'll figure out how to change this foolish substance into a positive human substance. Along these lines, you'll become a quiet and self-assured individual. This is a safe and ensured treatment that you can totally trust in light of the fact that your PCP is the shrewd oblivious personality that never commits errors. You'll likewise build up your insight by utilizing every one of your abilities. At the present time, a considerable lot of your unprecedented gifts have a place with your wild soul, which involves the greatest piece of your mind. You should figure out how to utilize your whole cerebrum and how to control your conduct before losing your brain. You just need to pursue the oblivious psychotherapy in your own fantasies.Understudies whose ADHD debilitates their learning may fit the bill for a custom curriculum under the Individuals with Disabilities Education Act or for a Section 504 arrangement (for kids who don't require specialized curriculum) under the Rehabilitation Act of 1973. Kids with ADHD can profit by study abilities guidance, changes to the homeroom arrangement, elective showing methods, and an adjusted educational plan

www.ingramcontent.com/pod-product-compliance
Lightning Source LLC
Chambersburg PA
CBHW031058250726

48655CB00004B/1495